Golders Green Synagogue

THE FIRST HUNDRED YEARS

Golders Green Synagogue

THE FIRST HUNDRED YEARS

For Vivienne and Jeffery,

Very best wishes

Helen Fry

HELEN FRY

Foreword by Rabbi Lord Jonathan Sacks

HALSGROVE

First published in Great Britain in 2016

British Library Cataloguing-in-Publication Data
A CIP record for this title is available from the British Library

ISBN 978 0 85704 280 4

HALSGROVE

Halsgrove House, Ryelands Business Park,
Bagley Road, Wellington, Somerset TA21 9PZ
Tel: 01823 653777   Fax: 01823 216796
email: sales@halsgrove.com

Part of the Halsgrove group of companies
Information on all Halsgrove titles is available at: www.halsgrove.com

Printed in China by Everbest Printing Co Ltd

Contents

The publication of this book has been made possible by generous donations from

Peter and Jacqui Zinkin, in loving memory of their fathers David Zinkin and Quentin Nisse

and

The Manuel family, in loving memory of grandparents Adelaide and David Manuel and their sons Lionel, Michael and Julian, in honour of their many years of collective service to Golders Green Synagogue

Appreciation is also expressed for a donation from the Glatman family in loving memory of Sydney Glatman and for a generous grant from the United Synagogue

Acknowledgements

THIS BOOK WOULD not have been possible without the immense support and enthusiasm of many people who provided material and photographs for this community history. I wish to offer my sincere thanks to Julia and Benny Chain, Peter Zinkin, Paul Morland and Jeremy Manuel who coordinated and organised aspects of the writing of the book at various stages and provided invaluable support to me. Paul Morland and Julia Chain read every chapter and offered indispensable advice on the material. However, any errors which may remain in the text are my sole responsibility. Every effort has been made to correct errors, however if any are brought to my attention, they can be amended in a subsequent edition of the book.

I am extremely grateful to Lord Sacks for generously writing the Foreword, and to the current Rabbi, Dr Harvey Belovski for his help and willingness to be interviewed, to Dayan Ivan Binstok for material, and to The United Synagogue for generously supporting the project in so many ways.

Huge thanks, too, must go to Brian Beckman, Jackie Crossley, Peter Zinkin, Professor David Latchman, Alan Mays and Maurice Samuelson for lending material and papers that are not in the synagogue's archives. Joel Clark, who edits the community magazine, has generously provided photographs relating to the community's most recent history.

A number of others also agreed to be interviewed for the book and/or provided additional material not available elsewhere. I am very grateful to all of them: Mrs Barbara Michaels (daughter of Rev. Livingstone) for her memories which stretch back to the 1920s; Mrs Naomi Rose who recalled the period of the shul's history from the 1930s onwards; Ken Craig (grandson of Rev. Livingstone); Rev. Rex Morton of St Alban's Church, Golders Green for material from the church's archives; Winston Newman, Rabbi Michael Newman and Adele Friedwald (children of Rabbi Dr Newman) for photographs and biographical information; Anthony Lytton for photographs and material on his grandfather, Rev. Asher Littenberg; Dr Rob Ginsburg; Lord and Lady Palmer; Lynn Fertleman; Dr Simon Cohen for material from his private collection; Julia Franks for material relating to the shul and her own family; Jonathan Davies; Shlomo Katanka for photographs and material about his father, the late Rabbi David Katanka; Terry Sopel for photographs relating to his father-in-law Leslie Green; Edna Martin; Charles Clore, Paul Burgess and David Lang; Ray Temple; Dr Michael Jolles for information on the rabbis and cantors from his vast research; Alan Cohen for material relating to Moss Reginald Levy in WW1; Sarah Kendal; Jonathan Gordzinski for photographs of the family bakery; and Helen Vegoda for photographs relating to her father Harry Ward.

This history has been enhanced by the generous help of Hugh Petrie, Heritage Development Officer at Hendon Library & Local Studies, who provided material and photographs from the Borough's collection relating to Golders Green throughout the decades.

The Golders Green Synagogue and I owe our grateful thanks to Simon and the staff at Halsgrove for agreeing to publish this history in a challenging record time, and for producing such a high quality book.

Thanks to my dear friend and mentor Rev. Elkan Levy for his continued support of my work and for providing some anecdotes about the community at Golders Green. Finally, my special thanks to Trudy Gold without whom I would not have been introduced to the Golders Green Synagogue; and to my ever supportive family.

Foreword

ELAINE AND I send our blessings and best wishes to the members and friends of the Golders Green Synagogue on this joyous centennial celebration of the community and we are honoured to have been invited to include our memories in this centenary commemorative book.

For us, this is a special and personal simcha. Between 1978 and 1982, we were Rebbetzen and Rav of the congregation and we have many warm and vivid memories of those days. For me it was the first United Synagogue in which I ever prayed on a regular basis, having been brought up in a series of *shteiblech*, and for some years in a Federation synagogue. It was, to put it mildly, a culture shock. I had to learn new tunes for all the davening. It was the first time I had ever heard shul music in the major key. *Litvisch shteiblech* tended to prefer the "Oy vey" school of Jewish music, sad, melancholy, and plaintive. Shul music in the major key sounded very English, very assimilated.

I had always felt, though, that the United Synagogue was something rare and special in Jewish life. It was inclusive, tolerant, generous in its embrace, and non-judgmental in its approach. Even then, these were unusual phenomena in the Jewish world, very necessary and spiritually uplifting.

What was so impressive was the intense loyalty the members of the community had for the shul and its traditions. Often I felt deeply humbled to be the Rav of such a congregation. There are many faces from those days that we miss today: they are davening for us in heaven. Many were deeply cherished friends and we miss them, even as we delight in rejoining the community thirty eventful years later and renewing other friendships

Elaine remembers our early years in Dunstan Road with great warmth, and how our children, then young, were welcomed into the community. One especial memory was the formation of the 3Gs, the Golders Green Group, and how we would, in groups, take it in turns to cook a fine meal in the shul kitchen and then enjoy it together in the evening with a guest speaker. The whole experience built friendships and community feeling. We made good friends and kept up with them over the years and it has been a great delight to return to the community and renew those friendships.

For us, one of the warmest of memories was of Moshe and Ruth Kohn, who were the living embodiments of *hachnasat orchim*, hospitality to all members of the community, especially new members and visitors. From them I really learned what the sages meant when they said, "Greater is hospitality than receiving the Divine presence."

How, I used to ask, was anything greater than receiving the Divine presence? Then I realised that the text in Genesis 18 – which speaks of how Abraham and Sarah offered hospitality to three passers-by – describes the visitors as "men". Genesis 19, in which two arrive at the house of Lot, speaks of them as "angels". To Abraham and Sarah they appeared as ordinary humans, yet they treated them like angels. To Lot, they appeared like angels yet he treated them like ordinary people.

Moshe and Ruth honoured their guests as if they were angels. That is how I finally realised that what the sages meant was that true hospitality means sensing the Divine presence in the face of a stranger, which is greater by far than recognising the Shekhinah when it arrives dressed in official uniform as it were, appearing unmistakably as an angel.

Moshe and Ruth were the welcoming face of the community. Their Shabbat table was always filled with guests, and on Shabbat afternoons theirs was always "open house" for everyone, and everyone was made to feel at home.

Perhaps the most transformative thing that happened in those days was the Adult Education Programme. It was not the first of its kind – Rabbi Abraham Levy of the Spanish and Portuguese congregation in Lauderdale Road had already created a truly impressive programme of his own – but it was the largest and most ambitious in any United Synagogue in those days, and it generated a huge buzz of energy.

It is invidious to name names – there were so many who contributed to the life of the community and working with each was a privilege – but it would be wrong not to mention the enormous contribution of Brian Beckman who in those days seemed to be organising everything, not just the Education Programme but so much else besides.

That programme, continued so impressively by Rabbi, now Dayan Binstock, was a game-changer, not just for the Dunstan Road community but for the United Synagogue as a whole. We were all beginning to realise that a shul was not just a place where you went to *daven*. It was or should be a community centre, built around the three essential values of Torah, Jewish study, Avodah, prayer, and Gemillut Hassadim, acts of kindness.

It also had to engage in outreach. The days when people did what they did out of tradition alone – I belong to a certain kind of shul because that's what my parents did, and theirs before them – were over. Shuls could no longer sit back and wait for people to come. They had to go out to the people, offering them a spiritual and social experience that enhanced their lives. The United Synagogue as a whole has truly embraced that message, to the immense benefit of British Jewry.

It is delightful now for Elaine and I to enjoy the warm and inspirational leadership of Rabbi Harvey Belovski and Rebbetzen Vicki. The synagogue itself has of course been transformed. It is a deeply moving experience so see how many new and young families have joined the congregation and witness the number of children that now attend the shul and its children's service.

At the heart of this renewal has been the Rimon School, opened in September 2012. The school itself is most impressive, and its effects on the community have been even greater than the most optimistic could have envisioned. This is what a Kehillah should be: a community centred on a school. The world only exists, said the sages, in the merit of the sound of Jewish children studying Torah.

The Golders Green Synagogue was built by pioneers. The United Synagogue a century ago had already understood that it had to support nascent communities in new areas of Jewish residence. Once the infrastructure existed, other communities tended to follow, so Golders Green became, as it still is today, a busy, bustling, centre of Jewish life.

But let us, on this anniversary, remember those pioneers and the many people across the years who sustained and were sustained by the life of the congregation. From the time of the Mishkan onward, shuls have been built by the voluntary contributions of those whose spirit moved them to help create, on earth, in finite space, a home for the Divine presence. What we enjoy today exists because of what they built yesterday, and may we in turn be builders of the Jewish tomorrow.

Every fifty years, the shofar would be sounded in Israel in biblical times to announce the Jubilee, the year focused on the renewal of the Jewish nation and its rededication to high ideals. Still today in Philadelphia you can see the great symbol of American independence, the Liberty Bell, with its Jubilee inscription taken from parshat Behar, "Proclaim LIBERTY throughout all the land unto all the inhabitants thereof."

The Golders Green community now celebrates its second Jubilee looking younger, fresher, more vibrant, and poised for growth than it has done in many decades. Therefore we pray to God: *Chadesh yamenu ke-kedem*, "Renew our days as of old." May we give strength to the shul, and may the shul give strength to us.

Mazal tov! With blessings and best wishes,
Rabbi Lord Jonathan Sacks

Interior of the synagogue today.

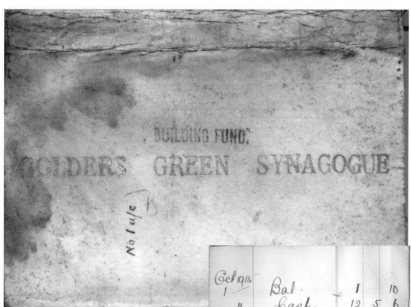

Building fund ledger 1915.

Interior of the synagogue today.

Introduction

THE GOLDERS GREEN Synagogue was the first purpose-built synagogue in a now cosmoplitan suburb. From small beginnings in 1915, it became a vibrant community with well over a thousand members at its peak. Writing the history of a community is a journey, a re-living of its triumphs and struggles, albeit at a distance of some years. At the start of writing this history of Golders Green Synagogue, one question was uppermost: why did a congregation start in the midst of a world war – the Great War? I soon discovered that the congregation's history is bound up with the history of Golders Green itself and the rapid expansion from open green fields to densely-populated urban development. Other questions emerged: who moved into the area and why? I soon discovered that this was an up-and-coming middle class area, and those Jews who moved there were coming, not primarily from the East End as one might expect, but from around Cricklewood and Kilburn.

In the 1910s, Golders Green was becoming a very sought-after area in which to live. However, research for the history of Golders Green Synagogue threw up something very unexpected. The religious life of the nascent Jewish congregation was bound up with another new community – the local Anglican Church of St Albans. From 1915, the Jewish community, which did not yet have its own purpose-built place of worship, rented St Alban's Hall from the local Anglican congregation. The hall had only been built in 1908, and was being used as the church. The local vicar, the Rev. Herbert Trundle, was himself in the throws of establishing a new congregation and trying to raise funds to build a proper church. And so I learned from its current-day vicar, Rev. Rex Morton, that St Alban's Church that one sees on North End Road today was not actually built until 1937 – at least fifteen years after the Golders Green Synagogue was consecrated.

In the early decades of these two communities, until the Rev. Trundle's death in 1937, the first minister of the Golders Green Synagogue, the Rev. Isaac Livingstone, and the Rev. Trundle had a close working relationship of cooperation and respect – all this in the days before the new relationship in Jewish-Christian dialogue. The renting of St Alban's Hall as a place for Jewish services from 1915 until 1922 was not an insignificant timespan in the history of the Golders Green Synagogue. The two congregations

Exterior, Golders Green Synagogue, 1927.

Interior, 1927.

coexisted with the Anglican Christian community worshipping in St Alban's Hall on Sundays and its major festivals, and the congregation of Golders Green Synagogue on Friday nights, Saturday mornings and all its festivals. The current incumbent, the Rev. Morton, showed me an old photograph of St Alban's Hall from 1915 and this is perhaps the most extraordinary discovery of all. From 1913 until the completion of the main church in 1937, St Alban's Hall was not a plain hall devoid of symbols. It was a highly decorated 'high church' with lots of Christian symbols and wooden pews. It soon became apparent that every week the Jewish community would have had to cover up the high altar, crosses, icons and symbols for its services.

Another surprise discovery in writing this book was to learn why it took so long for the synagogue to be built in Dunstan Road. This was the midst of the Great War and the government was using the plot as an allotment to 'feed the nation'. These gems in the synagogue's history are fascinating and underpin just how interesting local history can be.

The task of writing this history was made much simpler by the fact that the synagogue has kept a substantial archive that includes thousands of papers and correspondence since its foundation in 1915. The first Minute Book survives from July 1915 and all subsequent Minute Books until the 1990s, when records became computerized. The

congregation holds all Marriage Registers dating back to the first wedding solemnized in 1919 and also bar mitzvah/bat mitzvah records. This archive tells a very important history, without which, and with the passing of eyewitnesses to its early years, it would not have been possible to reconstruct. Whilst the community, quite rightly, serves the present needs of the growing congregation and looks to the future, the preservation of these records is absolutely vital. They provide a relatively complete picture of the rise, decline and revival of an important Anglo-Jewish congregation. These archives are irreplaceable records and some thought should go into deciding where best to deposit them for posterity. Many London synagogues are depositing their papers, alongside the Chief Rabbi's archives, Board of Deputies and Beth Din archives, at the London Metropolitan Archive near Farringdon.

The story of Golders Green Synagogue is primarily about the people – the lives of those who settled locally and shaped the community, keeping to its traditions and handing on that religious life to the next generation. This book is not just about the written history of the congregation, but also a pictorial record of the congregation from a wide range of photographs gathered from disparate sources. These, too, tell their own story of the first hundred years of the Golders Green Synagogue.

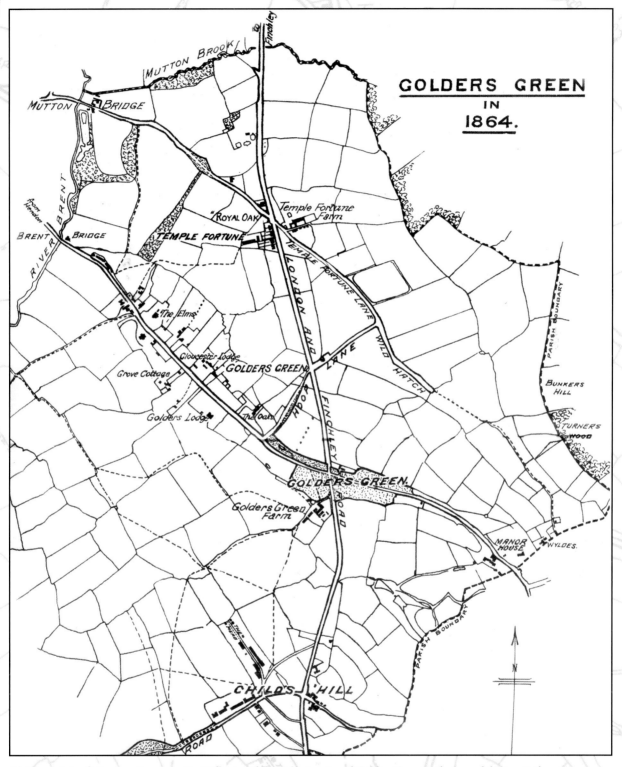

Above and the following 2 pages: *Maps showing the rapid expansion of Golders Green at the turn of the twentieth century.*

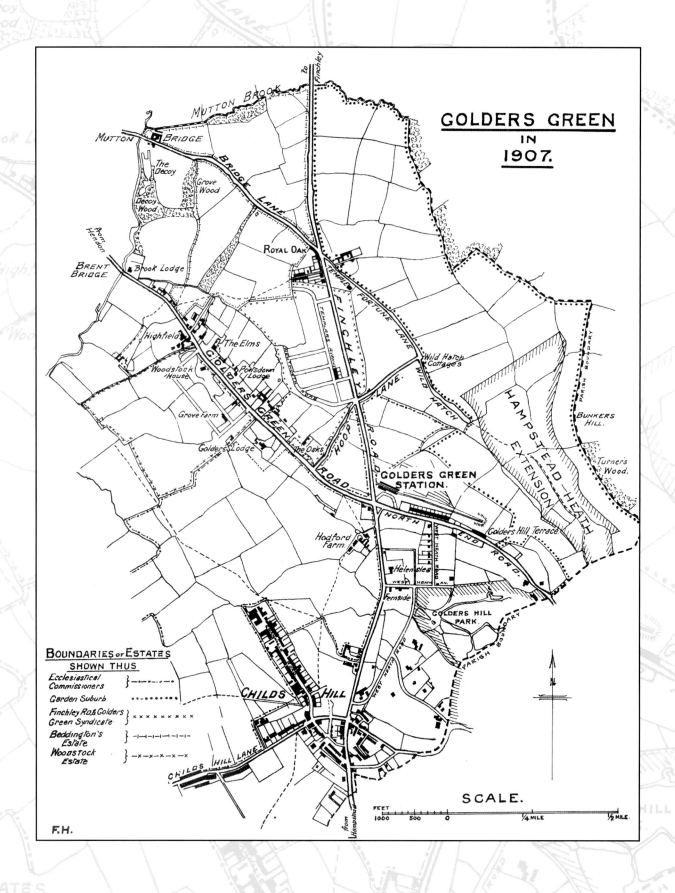

GOLDERS GREEN
IN
1907.

BOUNDARIES OF ESTATES
SHOWN THUS

Ecclesiastical
Commissioners
Garden Suburb
Finchley Rd & Golders
Green Syndicate
Beddington's
Estate
Woodstock
Estate

SCALE.

F.H.

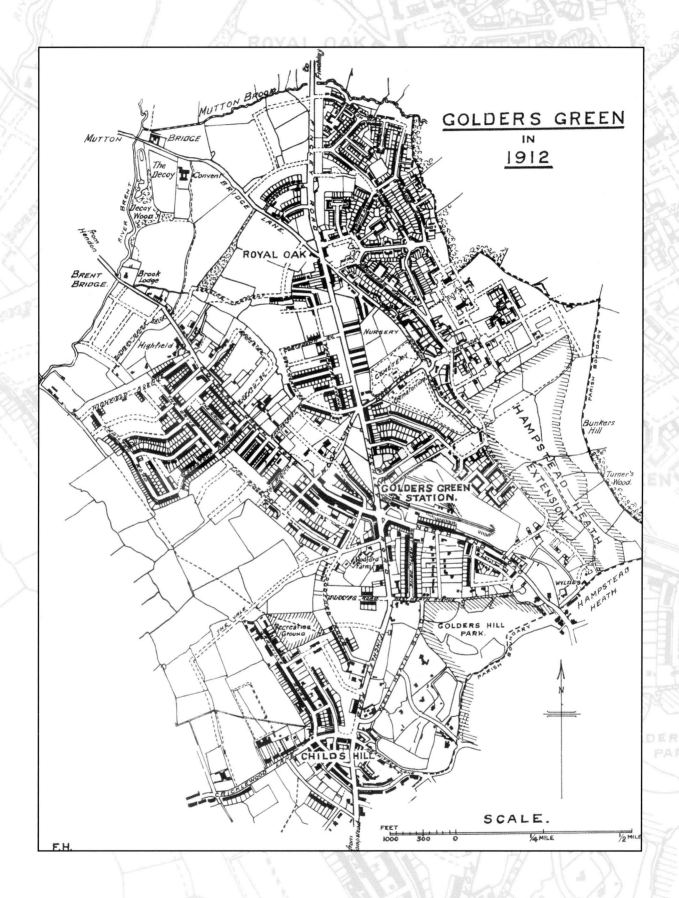

CHAPTER 1
Foundations of the Community

THE FIRST JEWISH community in Golders Green was formally established in 1915, just a year into the Great War. It was a congregation that would become known as the 'Golders Green Synagogue'. Until the turn of the twentieth century, Golders Green comprised mainly open fields with a total population of only around 300 people. A modest area then, its main industry was brick making. It also had a laundry and small hospital for children with skin diseases. The Jewish Cemetery in Hoop Lane was opened in 1897, followed in 1902 by the now well-known crematorium opposite. In 1892, Parliament had given authorisation for the expansion of the London underground from Charing Cross to the fields of Golders Green. The coming of the railway was significant because it precipitated further development in and around the Finchley Road, Temple Fortune and Child's Hill areas. With extra demand for housing for the increasing London population, expansion into Golders Green became

inevitable and, within two or three years, was rapid. Development of Golders Green took off from 1905 with plans for a tram route from Finchley to Cricklewood and the widening of the Finchley Road. The trigger for all this rapid development was the opening of the underground station in 1907. From 1910, trams began to operate here, until 1936 when they were replaced by trolley buses.

The year 1905 saw the construction of the first new house on the corner of Hoop Lane and Finchley Road. Two years later, in 1907, land originally belonging to the Eton College Trustees was purchased for the development of Hampstead Garden Suburb. The finance for the project was raised by Dame Henrietta Barnett, wife of Canon Barnett (founder of Toynbee Hall) whose vision of a 'garden suburb' was realised in her plans and design that still exists today, protected by the Hampstead Garden Suburb Trust. Barbara Michaels, daughter of Rev. Isaac Livingstone, one of the first ministers of the new community, recalls: 'The top of

View of the crossroads in the centre of Golders Green, 1906. Part of the triangular grassed area on the left is now the site of the clock tower, war memorial. COURTESY: HENDON LIBRARY & ARCHIVES

Golders Gardens where we lived was still open fields and undeveloped when I was a child. It was very different from the Golders Green of today.'

Golders Green Road soon became a smart shopping area, described as having 'the finest shops outside the West End of London.'[1] By now, it was an established, thriving middle-class area. In 1913, the famous Hippodrome opened, once home to the BBC Concert Orchestra. That same year saw the opening of the Golders Green Police Station in Temple Fortune, now sold for redevelopment. At the turn of the twentieth century, much of the land in this area was owned by Church Commissioners, and it was from this ecclesiastical body that the embryonic congregation of the Golders Green Synagogue eventually purchased its plot of land in Dunstan Road to build the first purpose-built synagogue in Golders Green.

First Religious Services

The rapid growth of London's Jewish community came in the 1880s with an influx into the East End of refugees from the pogroms of Eastern Europe. However, by the turn of the twentieth century, most of the Jews who came to Golders Green moved, not from the East End as expected, but primarily Willesden and Kilburn. They wished to

Ionic Theatre, 1915. COURTESY: HENDON LIBRARY & ARCHIVES

move to the leafier suburbs near Hampstead. In 1913, Jews living in Golders Green began to meet informally for services; and the first Rosh Hashanah services for this nascent community was held in the hall of the Middlesex Auto-Car Company in Heath Drive. Two years later, a meeting was held on Sunday 18 July 1915 at the Ionic Theatre, now the site of Sainsburys on the Finchley Road. The purpose of the meeting was driven primarily by educational concerns, in order to provide religious education for local Jewish families and continuity of Jewish tradition. It was acknowledged that a synagogue should be established for a place of worship.

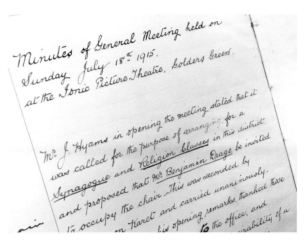

First entry in the Minute Book, Golders Green Synagogue, July 1915.

That Sunday in July 1915 marked the beginning of the formal establishment of the Golders Green Synagogue. The meeting was opened by Joseph Hymans and chaired by Benjamin Drage, the latter a businessman with a large furniture store in High Holborn.[2] During the course of the meeting, Drage was officially elected chairman of the 'Golders Green Synagogue'. In his opening remarks, Drage reiterated the need for a synagogue and religion classes to meet the religious needs of the growing Jewish population in the area. The Minute Book records the names of others who were present: Rev. Harris Cohen, Rev. Stolloff, Mr J. Victor, Paul Goodman, Mr H. Brown, Mr L. Bernstein, Mr Katz, Sol Karet, Mr Samuels and Mr Gollaney. All were united in supporting the aims of the meeting. Mr J. Victor, who voiced the need for a temporary place for worship, offered the loan of a Sefer Torah.

The decision to form a congregation was unanimous and it was agreed to establish a committee to deal with the formal establishment of the new community. The following were appointed to the committee: Benjamin Drage: president, Mr J. Victor: vice-president, Sol Karet: treasurer, and George Cohen and Joseph Hyams as joint secretaries. Additionally elected to a main body of the committee were

---

[1] *The Story of Golders Green*, p.39.
[2] During the 1930s, Benjamin Drage became a member of West London Synagogue and served as warden in 1931-3. He went on to render exceptional service to Anglo-Jewish causes and received a knighthood. In 1945, he gave over his home at Weir Courtney, Lingfield, rent-free to the Central British Fund for Jewish Relief and Rehabilitation for child survivors.

Mr H. Brown, Mr L. Bernstein, Mr R. Katz, Mr J. Davis, Mr E. Friedberg, Mr. R. Enoch, Mr P. Goodman, Mr M. Greidinger, Mr J. Samuel, Mr H. Lush and Jimmy Seaford. It was also decided to form a ladies canvassing committee, consisting of Mrs G. Cohen, Mrs B. Drage, Mrs J. Hyams, and Mrs Enoch. Those present were asked for donations, resulting in a collection of £162. 12s. 6d. being promised towards opening funds. In his concluding remarks, Mr Drage said: 'the movement was a splendid vindication of the Might, Majesty and the Beauty of Judaism, that at a moment when nation was clutching nation by the throat, we Jews and quiet Golders Green should be gathered together to the glorification and unity of our ancient faith.'

Two days later, another meeting was convened at Aysgarth, Woodstock Road, the home of Benjamin Drage, attended by H. Brown, J. Bernstein, R. Katz, J. Davis, P. Goodman, J. Samuel, J. Victor, Sol Karet, George Cohen, Joseph Hyams, H. Lush and Jimmy Seaford. They agreed to open the congregation's first bank account with the *London and South Western Bank* in Golders Green, in the name of 'the Golders Green Synagogue'. Pledges of just over £162, raised two days earlier, were deposited in the new account and formed the nucleus of a Building Fund; the original ledger of which still exists in the synagogue's archives.

It was agreed that the synagogue would be formed along the lines of the United Synagogue, although the new community was not accepted as an associate member of the United Synagogue until 1916. Jimmy Seaford and Mr H.

The original Minute Book of 1915.

Below: *Record of the first meeting that established the synagogue, July 1915.*

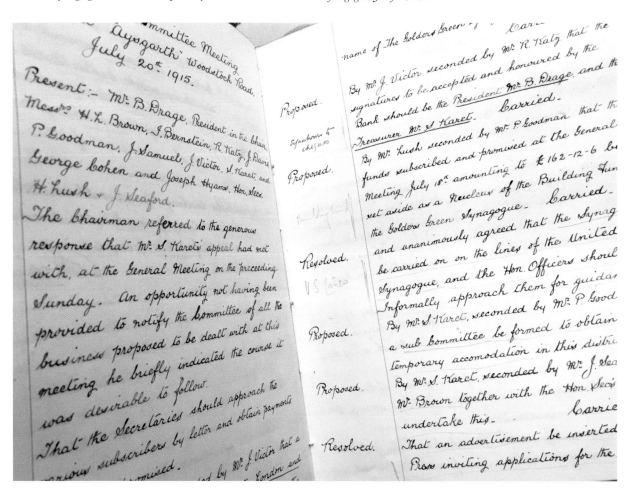

Brown formed a sub-committee to find suitable temporary premises, and an advertisement was placed in the Jewish press for the position of temporary reader. The ladies formed a Ladies Committee, tasked with setting up religion classes for children over the age of six and obtaining information on how many boys and girls in the area could be signed up for classes. The committee was offered assistance in the foundation of the new community from the Hampstead Synagogue and its minister, Rev. A. A. Green who 'will hold himself at your disposal for any assistance we can render you in connection with any of the above mentioned praiseworthy objects.'

A subsequent meeting of the new committee took place on 10 August at St Alban's Hall in North End Road, premises which belonged to the local congregation of the Church of England. During this meeting, the president offered a vote of congratulations to Mr and Mrs Brown on the celebration of their 50th wedding anniversary.[3] St Alban's Hall was soon to become the congregation's temporary place of worship from 1915 until 1922, and marked the beginning of an extremely fruitful relationship of cooperation and understanding between the two communities. George Cohen corresponded with the local vicar, the Rev. Herbert Trundle, about the terms of rental. It was agreed that it could be rented to the Jewish community for synagogue services initially on the basis of one year, effective from 4 September 1915.

This local Christian community was also newly formed,

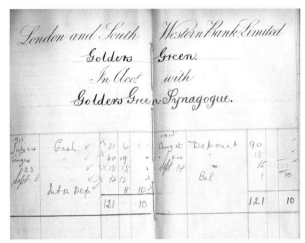

Building Fund ledger, first page, 1915.

being established in 1908 when St Alban's Hall was built. As its first vicar, the Rev. Herbert Trundle had been given the task of setting up a new Christian community in Golders Green at a time when the local population was still modest. The embryonic Christian congregation worshipped in St Alban's Hall until a purpose-built church was completed in 1937. The church was built on the site of a pond, once completely surrounded by farmland, as seen in an old engraving.[4] The foundation stone for the church was not laid until 1932. Completed in April 1937, under the architect Sir Giles Gilbert Scott, Rev. Trundle had

St Alban's Hall where synagogue services took place 1915–1922. All Christian symbols would have been covered up for the Jewish services. COURTESY: REV. REX MORTON

[3] Mr H. Brown was active in the community and in August 1916 was appointed to represent the Golders Green Hebrew classes at the Union of Hebrew & Religion Classes.
[4] Reproduced in *The Story of Golders Green*.

managed to raise £115,000 to build it debt-free during the height of the Depression. It was quite an achievement, but something that took its toll on his health and he died at the age of 62 later that same year.

What emerges during this period of almost a decade is the establishment of two parallel new congregations, one of which worshipped in St Alban's Hall on Friday nights and Saturday mornings, and the other on Sundays. They co-existed with tolerance and acceptance of each other's traditions and religious practices.

With the High Holy Days looming, the committee wrote to the Hampstead Synagogue in Dennington Park Road, asking for the loan of two Torah scrolls for the festivals. In preparation of the High Holy Days, letters were sent out to all known Jewish residents in the Golders Green district, inviting their support for the new congregation and offering a seat at services. The Minute Book records the price of seat rental for the High Holy Days from 10/6 to £2. 2s. 0d. depending on the seat, and a half rate for the ladies. Preparations also included a few minor renovations to St Alban's Hall and purchase of necessary furniture at a cost of £10. In accordance with the agreement with the Rev. Trundle, 'the whole of the furniture and property belonging to the synagogue be insured against Fire and Burglary for a sum of £100.'[5] A tenancy agreement was drawn up for the use of St Alban's Hall for services at £1 per week, plus 5/- per week when heating and lighting was used. The rent was set to rise to £4. 15s. 0d. a week for each of the Jewish festivals.[6] The long-term goal was always to erect its own purpose-built synagogue. By September 1915, the congregation had £120 in the Building Fund.

The consecration of the new temporary synagogue and the first Ma'ariv (the evening service) was set for Friday 3 September 1915. A public meeting subsequently took place at St Alban's Hall on Sunday 5 September at 3.30 p.m. in the presence of the Chief Rabbi Dr Hertz, and also attended by honorary officers of the United Synagogue and members of the Hampstead Synagogue. Advertisements about the first service and consecration were placed in the *Jewish Chronicle*.[7]

In late September, the Committee agreed to pay £21. 19s. 0d. to 'Percy, builder for arc (sic) and platform, and £13 for general repairs.'[8]

Selecting a Reader and Increasing Membership

With a temporary place of worship secured, a drive was undertaken to increase membership from Jewish residents in the vicinity, some of whom may not yet have heard about the new community. A new committee, the Canvassing

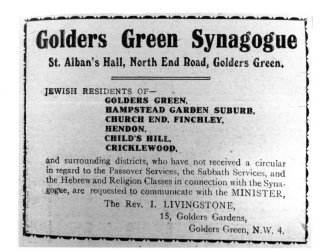

Advertisement in the Jewish Chronicle.

Committee, was formed to draw up a list of local Jewish residents who could be visited to explain about the new congregation. About membership, it was decided that: 'The minimum charge for men should be 21/- and women 10/6, with the usual United Synagogue assessments for Burial Rights and other charges.'[9] Occasionally, when it was not possible to rent St Alban's Hall if the Anglican congregation needed it for their own function, the Jewish community took up the offer of Miss Chapman's house for Saturday morning services.[10]

The congregation turned its attention to appointing its first reader. A number of candidates applied for the post. The community unanimously appointed Rev. Miller on a salary of £15 per annum. However, the appointment of a second reader provoked some disagreement. Having decided to engage Mr P. Schloss at a fee of £6. 6s. 0d., his appointment was suddenly cancelled and the Rev. Nathan Levine appointed in his place as temporary reader and minister:[11]

'At a weekly salary of 21/- and that he be required to attend on Friday evenings at sunset, Saturdays and all Holidays, and to preach from time to time, also for services on Mondays and Thursday mornings and on such other occasions as he may be called upon. The appointment to be subject to one clear week's notice on either side and to commence from Saturday October 2nd 1915.'

Just after taking up office on 2 October, the committee agreed to increase Rev. Levine's salary by 5/- a week.[12]

At the first meeting in January 1916, the congregation's bank account was reported as overdrawn,

---

[5] Minute Book entry for the meeting on 22 August 1915.

[6] Tenancy Agreement dated 8 September 1915.

[7] *Jewish Chronicle*, 27 August & 3 September 1915.

[8] Meeting, 26 September 1915, held at St Alban's Hall at 11am. Summary of the meeting in the Minute Book.

[9] Meeting held on 28th October 1915 at 'Aysgarth', Woodstock Road.

[10] Rev. Trundle received a letter from the secretary, enclosing a cheque for £6. 0. 0. for rental of the hall for the month of January 1916.

[11] Decision taken at a meeting held on 26 September 1915.

[12] Meeting, 10th October 1915.

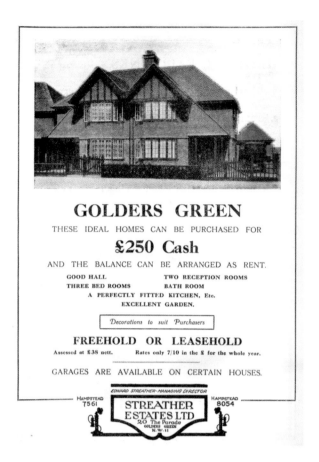

GOLDERS GREEN

THESE IDEAL HOMES CAN BE PURCHASED FOR

£250 Cash

AND THE BALANCE CAN BE ARRANGED AS RENT.

| GOOD HALL | TWO RECEPTION ROOMS |
| THREE BED ROOMS | BATH ROOM |

A PERFECTLY FITTED KITCHEN, Etc.
EXCELLENT GARDEN.

Decorations to suit Purchasers

FREEHOLD OR LEASEHOLD

Assessed at £38 nett.   Rates only 7/10 in the £ for the whole year.

GARAGES ARE AVAILABLE ON CERTAIN HOUSES.

EDWARD STREATHER · MANAGING DIRECTOR

| HAMPSTEAD 7561 | STREATHER ESTATES LTD 20 The Parade GOLDERS GREEN N.W. 11 | HAMPSTEAD 8054 |

Finances were again the subject of the next meeting on 16 January 1916, the main item described as 'Future Policy', 'the necessity of obtaining the necessary funds and the support to justify the selection of a site and the erection of a temporary building in the first place, to be followed in due course by a permanent synagogue.' Benjamin Drage wrote to Leopold de Rothschild offering him the chairmanship of the Building Committee. Rothschild agreed on condition that the synagogue was accepted into the United Synagogue. An application was submitted to the United Synagogue to become an associate synagogue, which was subsequently approved.[14] The congregation needed to raise more funds. Mr H. Brown offered £100 on condition that others could match it, and the sum of £100 each was promised by Benjamin Drage, Mr. Friedberg and Mr. Lush, raising a total of £400 of the £1000 needed.

By the following month, numbers for Saturday morning services started to improve. During Passover 1916, the congregation engaged the services of Rev. Michaelson for a payment of £5 5s. 0d and it was agreed to appoint a minister and teacher of religion classes at a salary of not more than £150 a year.[15] A number of minsters were invited to take services with a view to their suitability for the post. This same year, the community founded the *Golders Green Orphan Aid Society* to help the Jews' Hospital and Orphan Asylum. Throughout its hundred-year history, charitable causes were always central to the congregation's work.

Further pledges were made to the Building Fund: from Sol Karet - £15. 15s. 0d. Jimmy Seaford - £10. 10s. 0d. and Mr. Greidinger - £25. In addition, for the annual maintenance of the synagogue, Mr J. Samuels offered £5. 5s. 0d., Mr. Jacobs £5. 5s. 0d. and Mr Heiger £1. 1s. 0d. George Cohen tendered his resignation as Hon. Secretary and role taken over by Mr. Jacobs who, in a subsequent meeting, remarked 'upon the lack of decorum at the Sabbath services and the president promised that an attempt would be made to improve the same.'[16]

During 1916, religion classes for the youth were taught by Mr Supperstone and Mr J. C. Ellis of Jews' College, a temporary Reader at Brondesbury Synagogue. Classes continued to be held at St Alban's Hall. The committee was given the report of the *Union of Hebrew and Religion Classes* which inspected the religion classes on Sunday 28 July 1916. Its long report is taped into the Minute Book, part of which read:

'While there is ample provision for seating there are no desks or tables which is a serious drawback, for there is nowhere to rest the reading books and nowhere to write. There are 37 children on the roll. 27 were present on the day of the visit – a poor attendance. It is understood, however, that the average attendance is 33.'

with insufficient income to pay the weekly commitments of approx. £3. 2s. 0d. for rents and salaries.[13] Discussion ensued about the non-payment of seat rental by some members which had contributed to the problem. Mr Friedberg suggested that committee members defray the costs of the current expenditure of the synagogue and religion classes. Seconded by Mr Davis, the motion was carried. The following members agreed to pay the following amounts by quarterly installments until the Synagogue was able to finance its own commitments: Messrs. Benjamin Drage £20, H. L Brown £10, H. M. Lush £10, J. Davis £10, E. Friedberg £10, M. Greidinger £10, Jimmy Seaford 5-5-0, George Cohen 5-5-0, L. Bernstein 5-5-0, R. Katz 5-5-0, Sol Karet 5-5-0, J. Hymans 5-5-0 and P. Goodman 1-11-6. Other business discussed included the falling numbers in the religion school and the need to get the Ladies' Committee to canvas for new pupils. Saturday morning services would begin at 9.30 a.m., and Mr. Victor tendered his resignation as vice-president on health grounds. Benjamin Drage expressed, 'his personal appreciation of the earnestness and sincerity with which Mr. Victor had assisted in the early formation of the Congregation.' The Torah scroll which Mr. Victor had lent the congregation was to be returned because the United Synagogue had offered to loan one in its place.

[13] Meeting held on 9 January 1916 at 'Aysgarth', Woodstock Road.

[14] Entry in Minute Book, 12 March 1916.

[15] Mr. Goodman and Mr. Hieger were given the task of recommending a minister and teacher of religion.

[16] Meeting on 9 July 1916.

The age of the pupils ranged from 6 years to 13 years which made:

> 'instruction difficult owing to the impossibility of securing a proper age classification... The children are bright and keen and capable of going far. They read from the Prayer Book with their teacher, the reading was neither fluent nor correct. There is plenty of work to be done in that part of the teaching.'

Appointment of the Rev. Isaac Livingstone

The Board of Management met on 18 June 1916. Benjamin Drage reported that he had received: 'a letter from Rev. Livingstone offering his services for the vacant position of minister and it was now resolved that he be invited to officiate on Saturday next, June 24th and that the election of minister be left over until next meeting.' Rev. Livingstone was officially elected minister at a meeting of the Board of Management on 6 August 1916 and was inducted on the evening of Wednesday 27 September 1916.

He saw one of his first priorities as heightening awareness of the existence of the congregation in and around Golders Green. With that in mind, he took a street map and went from house to house knocking on any door with a mezuzah. Thus, he gradually encouraged an increase in membership and attendance at services. He once commented: 'I got hold of a directory, picked out the Jewish-sounding names and knocked on doors. I had some terrible disappointments, and I may have missed some Jewish Browns or Smiths.'

Rev. Isaac Livingstone.

Another pressing concern was the lack of a kosher butcher and delicatessen in Golders Green to meet the needs of the growing number of Jewish residents. Not long after taking up his position as minister, Rev. Livingstone corresponded with Messrs F. Barnett & Co, an East End kosher butcher, to persuade them to provide kosher meat for the Golders Green community. In a letter, he highlighted the fact that membership of his congregation now amounted to 120 households, with a further 100 families of non-members who, he believed, would join the congregation once the synagogue was built. He told Barnett & Co: 'Jewish families are coming into the district week by week, as quickly as houses are available. There is a very great need here for the very best class kosher butcher available for the supply of kosher meat.'[17] But it would be some time before Rev. Livingstone succeeded in persuading a kosher butcher to open a shop in the heart of Golders Green.

Rev. Livingstone was not only very active on a number of committees, but also founded many groups and clubs. By November 1916, he had established the popular Jewish Literary & Social Circle, of which he gave the inaugural lecture as its president, with Benjamin Drage serving as its first vice-president. Mrs Livingstone was also active within the community, especially with the founding of the Ladies'

Mr H. M Lushinski, warden 1922.

---

[17] Correspondence in the synagogue archives.

Guild, of which she was president. By the end of the year, Rev. Livingstone's duties were set to increase when the services of Mr Supperstone were terminated on a month's notice. Rev. Livingstone now took the religion classes after the Sabbath service. In addition, he was asked to take up the office of synagogue secretary and his salary increased to £200 per annum.[18] The services of Mr S. Ellis were engaged as assistant reader and teacher at a salary of £40 per annum.

Acquiring Suitable Land

During 1916, the Board of Management, led by Benjamin Drage, actively began the search for a suitable plot of land on which to build a synagogue. The services of architect Lewis Solomon & Son of Moorgate Station Buildings (EC2), the official architects to the United Synagogue, were engaged to advise on the suitability of land for sale in Golders Green. The more detailed task of finding the site itself, with price and other particulars, was delegated to an advisory committee, consisting of Mr Lush, Mr Brown and Mr Friedberg.

A freehold plot for sale in Templars Avenue (Temple Fortune) was the first site to be contemplated. The plot's frontage measured 105ft 2", and depth on one side 119ft 6", and on the other 119ft. Any building on site was to accommodate 400 male and 300 female worshippers, plus

Jimmy Seaford, a founding member.

a school room for between 80 to 100 children. Mr. Lush reported back that negotiations were still pending on the site, which was for sale at £840, with an additional £95-12-7 for road charges. In the meantime, Rev. Trundle agreed to rent St Alban's Hall to the congregation for another year for 25/- a week on a quarterly basis, and additional 20/- a day for festivals. Benjamin Drage wrote to Lewis Solomon & Son for advice on the site in Templars Avenue:[19]

> 'It is proposed in the first place to erect a building of a permanent nature at a cost of approximately £350 including furniture and fittings, to be used as a classroom or temporary synagogue, this structure must be erected upon a part of the site so that it will not obstruct or interfere with the erection of the permanent synagogue when we start building. If the site offered is not large enough for our purposes a decision on this point should not be delayed.'

Drage received a reply on 6 June that advised the site would be large enough, depending on whether the school was constructed in the basement or as a separate building at the side. But, he was informed, if the school rooms 'are to be in a separate building, as at Stoke Newington and Stamford Hill, and Dalston, the site is not large enough.' The approximate cost at pre-war prices of constructing a separate brick-built classroom building at the rear of the synagogue was estimated at £1,000, exclusive of sanitary accommodation, plus £100 for furniture and fittings.[20] The estimates were given at pre-war prices because it was impossible to provide an exact quotation during the wartime. In another letter, Lewis Solomon & Son advised:

> 'If you decide on a temporary building on the present site in Templars Ave, it will be necessary to pull it down directly you start to build the synagogue itself as it will be in the way of the new building, there not being sufficient room on the present site to erect a temporary building which will not interfere with the synagogue itself... Almost the whole cost (of the temporary building) will be wasted when we pull it down, as all the labour in the erection and fittings will be thrown away, and the old materials will not realize one-fourth of what they cost, and the only portion which will remain serviceable will be the seats and the drainage.'[21]

A site was also being considered in Finchley Road for the new building. The United Synagogue decided that 'the whole site with two frontages was much too large for the synagogue requirements.' The asking price was 'considerably more than should be given for the land on

---

[18] Meeting held on 2 November 1916 at 4 Park Rise, Finchley Road.
[19] Letter dated 31 May 1916.
[20] Letter from Lewis Solomon & Son to Benjamin Drage, 13 June 1916.
[21] Correspondence in the synagogue archives.

27

The Rev. Livingstone, from an oil painting.

which to build the proposed synagogue.' They considered the Templars Avenue end of the plot too small, and the Finchley Road part 'quite unsuitable'. They strongly urged that nothing further should be done in regard to the site.[22] The Board of Management agreed and decided not to proceed any further with it.

The next consideration was the purchase of the Wesleyan Church in Golders Green Road, but this had possible drawbacks, including passing traffic on the Golders Green Road and the underground being within a 100 yards. Even so, the president and committee considered it to be suitable and wrote to the United Synagogue to that effect. The Trustees of the Wesleyan Church met in January to discuss their situation and concluded:[23]

'No offer for the site could be considered that required the premises to be vacated during the war, and that their present building would not be vacated unless other and suitable premises for them were available.'

By January 1917, the balance of the Building Fund stood at £313.11.12. A site in Dunstan Road was now being considered as a possibility for the synagogue. In March

1917, Benjamin Drage asked Lewis Solomon & Son to comment its suitability. A reply was received on 19 March:

'We have considered the site at the corner of Hodford Road and Dunstan Road, and although the situation is good it is not large enough for the proposed synagogue if schools are to be a separate building from the synagogue itself... you will see that although the frontage is 135 feet, the depth at the back is only about 91 feet, and if you have the schools as well as the synagogue on that site it means excavating and putting the schools in the basement which will be both expensive and prevent us having a temporary building for use before the synagogue itself is erected... Not only is the site much narrower at the east end than at the west fronting Hodford Road, but we understand from the Hendon Urban District Council that they will ask us to set back 25 feet in a line with other houses in Dunstan Road which would make the land of considerably less value and quite useless for our purpose... If you can obtain the adjoining piece of land on which the foundations of two semi-detached houses have been built then the whole site would be very suitable for our purpose.'

A final decision as to which plot would be purchased by the community still had to be taken. In the meantime, Lewis Solomon & Son was asked to survey a site (130ft by 120ft) on the junction of Hodford Road and Helenslea Avenue.[24] Development on this site would require the synagogue building to be set back 25ft from each street, hence reducing the building to 105ft by 95ft. The site had insufficient space for a separate classroom building and would necessitate the classrooms being built in the basement, as in the case of Brondesbury Synagogue. Neither was there room on site for a good *succah*. The paving around the site, a requirement by the Council for this site, was estimated to cost in the region of £200 if the community decided to go ahead with the purchase of the land.

The congregation was still considering the Dunstan Road site which was emerging as the most suitable for a number of reasons. Importantly, it had sufficient land for classrooms to be built that could be used as a temporary synagogue whilst the main synagogue was being constructed. It also had sufficient land for any future expansion of the synagogue by extending the area behind the Aron Kodesh or Ark end in the same way as had happened at St John's Wood Synagogue.[25] But, as will soon become apparent, wartime had unexpected challenges for the new Jewish congregation.

[22] Meeting held on 26 November 1916 at 5 Laurel Bank.

[23] Reported in the Minute Book of the Golders Green Synagogue, 17 January 1917. Meeting held at Rev. Livingstone's house at 15 Golders Gardens.

[24] Letter from Lewis Solomon & Son to Benjamin Drage, 5 December 1918.

[25] Lewis Solomon & Son to Benjamin Drage, 20 December 1918.

CHAPTER 2
The Great War

THE NEW CONGREGATION felt the reality of war in a number of ways. Services were attended each week by soldiers from the Jewish Military Hospital at Tudor House, an auxiliary hospital in Golders Green. The congregation had its own members serving in HM Forces and arrears of seat rental for them were held in abeyance and charged as nominal members at a rate of £1-1-0 a year.[26] Those who lost their lives in action are commemorated on the War Memorial fountain in the vestibule of the current synagogue building. Those named from the Great War are: Pte Samuel Cohen, Flight Sergeant Jack H. Glass, Moss R. Levy, L/Cpl Stanley M. Levine and Sergeant Bernard Torrance (RAF). In the main synagogue there is a particularly poignant stained glass window that commemorates the sacrifice of one particular man. He was Moss Reginald Levy, attached to the Anson Battalion, 63rd Royal Navy Division who died in action near Cambrai in France in August 1918 at the age of only 19.[27]

The congregation was active in raising money for the war effort, in particular for the local military hospitals, the *Jewish War Victims Fund*, and the *Fund for the Care of the Sick and Wounded Soldiers*. In October the sum of £52.8.0 was raised for the *Fund for the Relief of the Jewish Victims of the War in Russia*.[28] Early the following Spring, a further donation of £26. 1. 6. was sent for the same fund. The sum of £4-10-0 was later raised for the Metropolitan Hospital Fund. The congregation continued to use St Alban's Hall for services and enjoyed a fruitful relationship with the local non-Jewish population. Weekly numbers in religion classes fell because of the air raids.

During 1916, Chief Rabbi Dr Hertz circulated a letter to synagogues suggesting a Service of Intercession for the War and a collection for the *Fund for the Care of the Sick and Wounded Soldiers*. And so, in December 1916, Golders Green Synagogue held a Service of Intercession, during which Rev. Livingstone called for donations to be made in aid of wounded soldiers. In response, a few days later, congregant and member of the Board, Mr H. Brown, wrote to Rev. Livingstone:

'I send you One and a half Guineas and with the Half Guinea I sent you before makes Two Guineas

Golders Green War Memorial.

Funds raised by the synagogue for the local military hospital.

---

[26] The Minute Book notes this in the case of George Cohen and J. Seaford, for example.

[27] Reginald Levy's service record is held in ADM 339/2/2705.

[28] Letter of thanks from Chas. E. Sebag Montefiore to Rev. Livingstone, 21 October 1916.

towards the Fund for our wounded sailors and soldiers for which you have held Intercession Service. I hope you have got from all the members their donations to this noble fund. If they are not true attendants at the synagogue I hope they will be loyal and patriotic subjects and support you in this effort of raising funds for those who have been unfortunate in being wounded and some of them crippled for life in this disastrous war.'[29]

Golders Green War Memorial.

Challenges in Wartime

Any hopes of beginning construction work on a new synagogue building soon were dissipated. This was wartime and the difficulties of building at such a time could not be underestimated. The architects, Lewis Solomon & Son, had warned the community that even erecting a temporary place of worship whilst the main building was under construction would prove difficult. Their reasons:

'Boarding has gone up in value by leaps and bounds, and corrugated iron which is the ordinary material

used for temporary buildings it is almost impossible to get at the present moment... We accordingly think you should not reckon anything less than £600 for the outlay on a temporary building, as this would have to include sanitary accommodation and drainage, also heating, lighting and seating. As to the time it would take to erect such a building, we cannot give you any idea at present as material is so scarce and labour also.'[30]

However, the congregation soon discovered from the engineer that, under the Cultivation of Lands Orders 1916–17, the Council had taken over the land temporarily for allotments to 'feed the nation', something which could be effective until at least September 1920. The community now faced the prospect of several years before any building work could commence on site. This did not deter the committee from continuing with the ultimate goal of a purpose-built synagogue, in spite of the huge challenges.

At a meeting of the Board, the synagogue finances were discussed. Income of £262-13-6. per annum now overtook expenditure of £252.[31] Details of Purim and Passover services were circulated to all Jewish households in Golders Green to raise attendance. The Board discussed whether Rev Livingstone could accept a position as officiating clergyman to the troops. The committee was completely split on this issue, with 4 votes for, and 4 against. The chairman gave the casting vote 'against' and the motion was lost. At an April meeting, the chairman referred to the regrettable loss that had fallen on the community by the death of the Rev. John Chapman: 'a courtly and kindly gentleman who added dignity to any assembly, & whose passing away left a blank not easily filled.'[32] No further details are given about Rev. Chapman or his precise links to the community.[33]

With regard to the building of the synagogue, 'the chairman gave further particulars in connection with the site at the corner of Hodford Road and Dunstan Road. Messrs Lewis Solomon and son had reported that in their opinion the site was an excellent one for the purpose required.'[34] The details of the site were referred to the United Synagogue, and a decision on its purchase deferred for a month. The United Synagogue informed the congregation that the land was suitable and 'worth the money, provided there are no special restrictive covenants.'[35]

The Minute Book records: 'A vote of condolence to the family of the late Mr Leopold de Rothschild, recalling the genial charm of the late philanthropist on the occasion of Mr Drage's visit to him in connection with the proposed

---

[29] Letter dated 1 January 1917.

[30] Letter dated 16 June 1916.

[31] Meeting held on 4 March 1917 at 'Aysgarth', Woodstock Road.

[32] Meeting held on 15 April 1917. A letter of condolence was sent to his family.

[33] An entry appears for him in *The Palgrave Dictionary of Anglo-Jewish History*. Early in his career, Rev. Chapman served as assistant minister at the Western Synagogue, and was later involved in Jewish education.

[34] Entry in Minute Book, 15 April 1917.

[35] Reported at the meeting held on 13 May 1917 at 'Aysgarth', Woodstock Road.

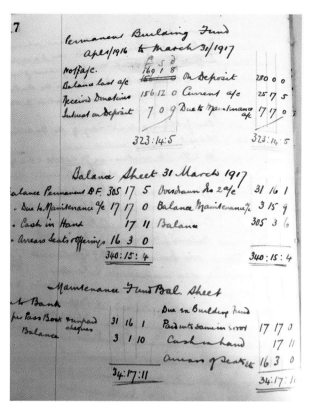

Extract from the Golders Green Synagogue accounts, 1917.

synagogue.'[36] Board member Mr Seaford tended his resignation because he had been called for military service.

Rev. Sydney Ellis, the assistant reader aiding Rev. Livingstone with Hebrew and religion classes, sent in a letter of resignation because he was about to take up appointment as Army Chaplain to the Jewish Forces in France. At the next meeting on 27 June, the committee received a request from Rev. Ellis to be reinstated as assistant reader because he had not been able to take up his position as Chaplain to the Jewish Forces. The meeting decided 'no', partly because it was felt that he could not fulfill both duties easily. However, because he had temporarily resumed duties, he was to be reimbursed for his time. An advertisement was placed in the *Jewish Chronicle* for his post:

> 'Applications are invited for the position of Teacher; one able to assist in reading the Sabbath services, if required, would be preferred. The classes are held on Sunday mornings only, from 10.30 to 12.30; salary £20 pa – Applications with qualifications to be addressed to Superintendent, the Rev. I. Livingstone, 15 Golders Gardens.'

In the end, a suitable candidate was not found and Rev. Ellis was unanimously reinstated 'for a period of three months from 1st September as assistant Reader and Teacher

at a remuneration of £10.'[37] Rev. Livingstone continued canvassing around Golders Green for new members. He referred to the necessity of providing four chairs for houses during *shiva*, the period of mourning. The chairman offered to procure six chairs for this purpose. Rev. Livingstone was now to be responsible too for the letting of seats. All seatholders for the main festivals were expected to enrol as regular members. Rev. A. A. Green accepted an invitation to preach on the second day of Rosh Hashanah. Meanwhile, Rev. Livingstone drew the attention of the committee to: 'one or two indications of a lack of decorum at some synagogue services and expressed the hope that they would help his efforts to make the services impressive and decorous.' The indications specifically mentioned were (i) the sitting down of some congregants during prayers like Alenu and Kaddish when it was customary to stand (ii) the custom of leaving the synagogue during the recital of the Memorial Prayers on the last days of Festivals.

With High Holy Days just months away, Rev. Livingstone wrote to Rev. Trundle of St Alban's Hall with a list of dates and times to reserve the hall for services, sometimes requiring the hall all day. Always accommodating, Rev. Trundle agreed to the list which comprised services on at least 10 consecutive days. It must be borne in mind that his own purpose-built church had yet to be erected. Ordinarily, St Alban's Hall was set up as High Church with Christian symbols and artifacts. Every time it was used for a Jewish service, all Christian elements

Golders Green Synagogue.

Temporary Address :
St. Alban's Hall, North End Road, N.W.3.

Minister		REV. I. LIVINGSTONE.

Honorary Officers :

President		BENJAMIN DRAGE, ESQ.
Vice-President		H. M. LUSH, ESQ.
Treasurer		S. KARET, ESQ.
Hon. Secretary		JOSEPH HYAMS, ESQ.

Committee :

L. BERNSTEIN, ESQ.	MONTAGUE JACOBS, ESQ.
A. BLOCH, ESQ.	R. KATZ, ESQ.
G. COHEN, ESQ.	H. KERMAN, ESQ.
J. DAVIES, ESQ.	L. LUBIN, ESQ.
S. DRAGE, ESQ.	J. M. MAURICE, ESQ.
PAUL GOODMAN, ESQ.	J. SAMUEL, ESQ.
M. GREIDINGER, ESQ.	J. SEAFORD, ESQ.
F. HIEGER, ESQ.	A. L. VICTOR, ESQ.

Services every Saturday at 10 a.m.
Classes (under the direction of the Minister) every Sunday at 10.30 a.m.
Festival Services announced by Circular.
Special Services can be arranged for.

---

[36] Meeting held on 15 July 1917.
[37] Minute Book entry, 1 August 1917.

had to be removed or covered up which took some considerable time.

When the committee met in November 1917, they were mourning the loss of founding member Mr H. Brown. The chairman referred in 'feeling terms to the loss sustained by the death of and moved that the deep sympathy of the Board of Management of the Golders Green Synagogue be extended to the wife and family of the late Mr H. Brown, and that the warm appreciation of his work for Judaism in general and the Golders Green Synagogue in particular be recorded in the minutes.'[38] After complaints previously about decorum in services, Benjamin Drage was able to report: 'the well attended services on the High Festivals exhibited a high standard of reverence and decorum, which he hoped the committee would do its utmost to maintain.' Rev. Livingstone's salary was raised by £50 per annum to £250 per annum. Rev. Sydney Ellis was reappointed yet again as assistant reader on the same terms as before, with three months notice on either side. The Ladies' Committee was asked to provide the prizes for Channukah prize-giving and tea for the children. A lengthy update ensued on how to proceed with a kosher butcher. Rev Livingstone explained that he had written to certain butchers to see if they would open a shop in Golders Green, with little success. Generally, numbers for Sabbath services had fallen again due to recent air raids, a constant reminder of the reality of the war.

At the end of November 1917, the committee agreed to send the following letter to Prime Minister Lloyd George, with a duplicate copy to the English Zionist Federation. It concerned the Balfour Declaration signed on 2 November:

'That this meeting of the Hon. Officers and Board of Management of the Golders Green Synagogue, held at Aysgarth, Woodstock Road on Wednesday November 28th 1917 places on record its heartfelt gratitude to His Majesty's Government for the close interest and concern they have shown towards the Jews.'

As the new year dawned on the final year of the Great War, Benjamin Drage, the congregation's first president, tendered his resignation on the ground that 'he did not feel fitted either by conviction or temperament to occupy a position which he held should only be filled by a good Jew who adhered to Orthodox Jewish observances.' He added that he would remain a member.

A lengthy discussion ensued amongst the committee who were united that it would be disastrous for him to resign at such a critical moment in the community's life. The resolution was unanimously agreed: 'that having received the resignation of Mr Benjamin Drage as President of the Golders Green Synagogue, this resignation be not accepted, and that its consideration be deferred until the next meeting.'[39] Finally, he agreed to stay on as president because, while his views had not changed, he recognised that 'his withdrawal might have a disturbing effect on the synagogue's efforts.'[40]

Odeon Cinema, Golders Green.,
COURTESY: HENDON LIBRARY & ARCHIVES

---

[38] Minute Book entry, 4 November 1917.
[39] Minute Book entry, 27 January 1918.
[40] Meeting held on 18 April 1918 at Rev. Livingstone's home, Golders Gardens.

A close account was kept on synagogue numbers. In particular, religion classes had risen from 36 pupils in December 1916 to 41 pupils in June 1917. However those numbers fell to 28 by October 1917 due to the air raids. By the following year, it steadily rose again to 34. It was noted that attendance at Passover services by members that year was disappointing.

High Holy Day and Yom Kippur services filled over 260 seats, but attendance at services during the rest of the year left much to be desired.

Charitable support was given to the local military hospitals and an appeal for funds generated a donation of £7-15-0 from the synagogue. Rev. Livingstone attended, too, a meeting of London synagogues, convened by the Society for the Protection of Girls and Women which sought to raise awareness and raise funds. Golders Green Synagogue raised £2-16-2, in addition to annual subscriptions of £1-16-6. Praise was given for the Ladies' Committee whose work was mainly taken up with 'the making of garments for necessitous institutions.'

The names of soldiers commemorated on Golders Green War Memorial.

A Plot for a Synagogue

The search for a plot for a synagogue continued and a site was yet to be purchased. The United Synagogue commented that the Building Fund was meager and the congregation did not have sufficient members to warrant the building of a large synagogue. Members of the Board of Management believed that membership was not increasing substantially, precisely because there was no purpose built synagogue. At this point, the community still had in mind to erect a temporary synagogue first, then build a permanent one next to it, using the temporary synagogue building eventually as the permanent school. With that in mind, a letter was sent to the Ministry of Munitions asking whether permission could be obtained to erect a building on land when purchased. There was yet

some bureaucracy to overcome. The Ministry of Munitions replied that it was necessary for the congregation to make a formal application for a Building License. For that, technical details were required, so Messrs Lewis Solomon & Son were asked to prepare a sketch of the classroom and temporary synagogue to be considered by the committee. Rev. Livingstone prepared a petition to be signed by Jewish households to be sent to the Ministry of Munitions stating that in the interests of the local community the erection of a temporary synagogue is 'an urgent necessity.'

To try to press forward with the building project, a meeting was held with Honorary Officers of the United Synagogue,[41] who agreed that Golders Green Synagogue could go ahead and undertake to find the costs of half the land and erection of a temporary synagogue. This would amount to £6,000. The United Synagogue undertook to lend the remaining amount of £3,000 and agree to the synagogue becoming a Constituent Synagogue. All administration and religious observance thereafter was to be subject to the supervision and control of the Chief Rabbi

Stained glass window in the synagogue, dedicated to Moss R. Levy who died in action in WW1.

[41] Reported in synagogue's Minute Book, 12 May 1918.

of the United Congregations of the British Empire:

> 'No persons or Reader at this synagogue to be appointed without the sanction of the Chief Rabbi. Nor shall any person conduct religious services or preach therein without the permission of the Chief Rabbi.'

Messrs Lewis Solomon & Co approached Hendon Urban District Council for permission to erect a temporary synagogue. Hendon Urban Council required drawings of the site, so the architects drew up plans at a cost to the synagogue of £5. 5s. 0d. In July 1918, generous donations were given to the Building Fund by Robert Waley Cohen (£26. 5s. 0d.), F. D Benjamin (£25), I. Passoff (£2. 2s. 0d.) and A. Davis (£1. 1s. 0d.). By the following month, over £900 had already been raised in the Building Fund. Of that amount, £450 was transferred to National War Bonds. The Ladies' Committee undertook various fundraising activities towards the Building Fund. By the end of 1918, the synagogue's general day-to-day finances were improving and the Building Fund accrued £919. 3s. 1d., with outstanding promises of £346. 16s. 0d. The sum of £850 was invested in National War Bonds. The United Synagogue inspected a plot at Dunstan Road.

Communal Life

The Minute Books and correspondence give a fairly detailed overview of the life of the community in these war years. There was praise from the Board of Management for the late Mr. H. Brown (vice-president for so long) for his 'devoted sustained energy and ability to the furtherance of every congregational effort'. It was noted that the synagogue was not yet registered for the solemnisation of marriages. Consequently, Rev. Livingstone was obliged to refer applicants to another synagogue or conduct the ceremony under the auspices of another synagogue. By 1918, membership of the synagogue had increased to 116 households. Rev. Livingstone continued his negotiation to persuade a kosher butcher to open in Golders Green. He and his wife became Organising Minister and Correspondent of the Rochelle Street School in Shoreditch that had nearly 400 pupils, one of the largest in the East End.

Various clubs and societies continued to thrive. The Golders Green Literary and Social Circle enjoyed good attendance at Lyndale Hall where they met regularly, rent-free. Rev. Livingstone was still its president, and Hon. Secretary was Mr N. A. Esserman. The children's annual prize distribution was held at Benmore Hall, addressed by Rev. Dayan H. M. Lazarus, and distributed by Mrs Drage. The Chief Rabbi wrote to congratulate Rev. Livingstone and his co-workers on the progress being made with work on the synagogue and congregation.

The synagogue's War Memorial fountain.

During 1918, Rev. Ellis resigned his position as reader and teacher for a second time; this time to take up a position at the Watford & Bushey Congregation. In a letter written to Rev. Livingstone, he said:

> 'I very much regret having to part from Golders Green where I have been fortunate in making many good friends and where more than any where else I had the opportunity of getting a sound ministerial training... To you personally I am indeed indebted for many things and I hope never to forget your kindness, advice and guidance.'[42]

---

[42] Letter to Rev. Livingstone, 20 August 1918.

Stained glass memorial window, Moss R. Levy.

The names of those commemorated on the synagogue's own War Memorial.

The problems for the community posed by his resignation were several. He had given just four days notice when his contract stipulated three months, and it came just 16 days before the High Holy Days with little hope of finding a replacement so soon. The Board complained by letter to the Watford & Bushey Congregation, and also to the Chief Rabbi. Rev. Ellis refused to reconsider his position. Several meetings ensued, but because Rev. Ellis was out of town, he did not receive the letter asking him to attend a meeting with the Chief Rabbi. Watford & Bushey Congregation responded to say that they would not have appointed Rev. Ellis if they had realized his obligations to Golders Green were for three months notice, and they had appointed him with immediate effect. After various deliberations, the Golders Green Synagogue decided not to take the case to its logical or legal conclusion. Consequently, no charges were brought against Rev. Ellis, but he had to forfeit a

month's salary. Over the High Holy Days, Lazarus Cohen was engaged as reader at Golders Green Synagogue.

The question of marriages was a relevant one for the community and as such, a request was sent to the Board of Deputies of British Jews for Rev. Livingstone to be registered for the solemnisation of marriages. This was granted in due course, and the first marriage solemnised in 1919.

On 11 November 1918, the guns fell silent across Europe and war was finally over. It had been a war of enormous sacrifice and horrific suffering on both sides. In the first committee meeting after the Armistice and held at St Alban's Hall, Benjamin Drage, who had led the community as its president throughout the war years, said: 'The day was an occasion of importance marked by an event of even greater importance – the coming of victory and the dawn of Peace.'[43]

---

[43] Meeting held 17 November 1918.

CHAPTER 3

The Synagogue

BY THE END OF 1918, the search for a suitable plot of land was almost over and it was no longer necessary to get permission from the Ministry of Munitions to build. The United Synagogue had inspected and approved the site at Dunstan Road, and architects Lewis Solomon & Son were instructed to 'proceed with the acquisition of the site and gain consent to test the soil'.

At a committee meeting held at Benjamin Drage's home on 22 January 1919, the site was officially approved by the Golders Green Synagogue. It was reported that the Ecclesiastical Commissioners were prepared to let the site for £45 per annum, with the purchase of the freehold after the synagogue had been built. The Minute Book records:

> 'That it is desirable to erect and found a Synagogue, to be known as the Golders Green Synagogue (as a Constituent Synagogue of the United Synagogue), in the district of Golders Green, for persons of the Jewish Religion who use the Ashkenazi ritual… the site and property known as Dunstan Road may be acquired for the purpose of the erection of the said Synagogue and Class Rooms… that the terms of the Building Agreement to be entered into with the Ecclesiastical Commissioners for England…'

On 11 February 1919, Golders Green Synagogue made a formal application to be admitted as a constituent synagogue of the United Synagogue, now serving 230 Jewish households in the area (not all of them members of the shul). The stipend of Rev. Livingstone was raised to £312 per annum. That autumn, his salary was increased from £312 to £416 per annum. The Golders Green Synagogue, still worshipping at the temporary premises of St Alban's Hall, was finally registered for marriages. A *chuppah* (canopy) for the marriage ceremony was needed, so the ladies of the congregation were asked to provide the covering for it. Benjamin Drage offered the fittings and agreed to order a book to register the Ketuboth or marriage certificates. The marriage fee was set at £3. 3s. 0d. in addition to half-year membership for non-members.

The first entry in the synagogue's Marriage Register is dated 26 October 1919 for the wedding of Solomon Lewis, a civil servant in the Admiralty, to Nathalie Neudorf, the daughter of a diamond merchant. They were registered as married in 'Golders Green Synagogue, St Alban's Hall', and officiated by Rev. Livingstone. The second entry took place almost nine months later on 9 June 1920, again officiated by Rev. Livingstone. This time, it was for the marriage of Maurice Katzner, a wholesale clothier, to Catherine Fuld,

they would receive sympathetic consideration in the event of the services of the Burial Society being required.' He received a reply to confirm:

'The granting of seatholders of the Golders Green Synagogue burial rights in the cemeteries of the United Synagogue at the rate of half a guinea per head per annum, subject to the acceptance of the names, until such time as the synagogue shall have been established as a Constituent Synagogue'.[45]

Fundraising for the Building Fund continued in earnest with a recital by Miss Lewisohn that raised £220, and Mrs Kay and Mrs Livingstone of the Ladies' Society organised dances and whist drives to raise £52. They also held a garden party. The total in the Building Fund had almost reached £1,500. The *cheder* (religion school) numbers had risen to 40 children. Amidst their own fundraising, the congregation did not forget the needs of others and Rev. Livingstone sent a letter to every member appealing for donations for Polish Jewry. The Polish Appeal raised £119. 14s. 6d., a not insignificant sum in 1919. The following year, £8. 5s. 0d. was raised for a Red Cross appeal.

the daughter of merchant, Julius Fuld, and took place at Frascati Restaurant in Oxford Street.[44]

Other rites of passage needed to be clarified too. For burial rights, Rev. Livingstone conferred with the United Synagogue because members at Golders Green had no burial rights whatsoever 'except that in accordance with the letter from the United Synagogue of 18 October 1916,

The synagogue decorated for Shavuot.

[44] Located at 32 Oxford Street in the West End.
[45] 21 October 1919

Dunstan Road Site

At a meeting on 9 April 1919, the terms for acquiring the site at Dunstan Road were presented to the committee. As soon as the synagogue was completed, the congregation had the option, at a cost of up to £2,400, to take out a lease for 99 years from Lady Day 1919 at £17 pa rent; £35 from Lady Day 1920, and £51. 10s. from Lady Day 1921 to 1922. Or the congregation could purchase the freehold before Lady Day 1924 for the sum of £1312. 10s. 0d. Trustees named on the contract of the new synagogue were Lionel de Rothschild,[46] Albert Morris Woolf, Robert Waley Cohen, Frank David Benjamin, Samuel Henry Emanuel, Arthur Lindsay Lazarus, Nathaniel Sampson Lucas, Samuel Moses, Benjamin Drage, Solomon Karet and Henry Maurice Lushinski.[47] Later in the year, Joseph Hyams' name was added to the list of trustees of synagogue with the approval of the United Synagogue.[48] The erection of the synagogue was entrusted to the Building Committee of the United Synagogue in consultation with the committee of the current Golders Green Synagogue. Lionel de Rothschild had been appointed chairman of the Building Committee.

Momentum and enthusiasm for the new site grew. Mr S. Criger of the New West End Synagogue offered to present the Golders Green Synagogue with a Torah scroll. Rev. Livingstone suggested that 'the offer be graciously accepted and that, as this was the first scroll to be presented to the synagogue, a service and reception be held to mark the occasion.'[49] With High Holy Days approaching, provision had to be made for an increased congregation for services, so 316 seats were reserved (198 male, 118 female), an increase of 102 seats on the previous year. Membership had increased to 265 adults (140 males, 125 females – representing 150 households). Offerings collected over High Holy Days amounted to £140. 8s. 0d.

By the end of the year, the congregation still faced challenges of raising sufficient monies for building a synagogue. A meeting of seatholders was convened at St Edward's Hall in Finchley Road, in which Benjamin Drage explained the progress and difficulties since the foundation of the congregation in 1915. He said that it had grown from a membership of just 20 in 1915 to 270 in 1919. Rev. Livingstone made a further appeal for the Building Fund, promising that the congregation would soon have its own building. Pledges received at the meeting totalled £700, bringing the total collection to date to nearly £4,000. Regular meetings took place with the United Synagogue to advance the progress of the synagogue building. By February 1920, the Building Fund amounted to £5,211.

The warm relationship between Rev. Livingstone and Rev. Trundle continued in the 1920s. This is illustrated

COURTESY OF MAURICE SAMUELSON

well by a letter from Rev. Livingstone to Rev. Trundle in February 1920:

> 'Remembering the generous and kindly thoughts you expressed when last the Chief Rabbi (the Very Rev. Dr J. Hertz) addressed our congregation at St Alban's Hall on Sunday September 5th, 1915, my Honorary Officers desire me to invite the honour of your company at a meeting of the seatholders of the synagogue which is being arranged for Sunday March 7th, on which date the Chief Rabbi has once again consented to be present. It will be interesting for you to know that the hospitality of St Alban's Hall which you so generously extend to my congregation has conduced substantially to the progress and the prosperity of the synagogue establishment. Starting with a membership of 20 in 1915 we now number close on 300 adult members.'

A second teacher for Sunday classes was to be engaged, on a salary of 'not more than £48 per annum and to train a choir after Shabbat morning service'.[50] Mr A. Supperstone accepted the appointment as assistant teacher for £55 per

---

[46] Lionel de Rothschild was the eldest son of Leopold de Rothschild who had been offered the chairmanship of the Building Committee of the Golders Green Synagogue in 1916. Leopold de Rothschild died the following year in 1917.

[47] Entry in Minute Book, 29 May 1919, meeting at Rev. Livingstone's home.

[48] Minute Book, 11 September 1919.

[49] 19 November 1919.

[50] Meeting held on 21 January 1920.

annum. Some members had favoured Mr. S. Michaels. The final decision was deferred, but eventually Mr S. Michaels was appointed as assistant teacher and choirmaster at a salary of £75 per annum.

The sums involved in constructing a synagogue in the 1920s were not insignificant. Estimates were put to the committee. The cost of building the first section of the synagogue would amount to £20,000, inclusive of heating, lighting, the Aron Kodesh (Ark) and Almemar (space in front of the Ark), but excluding furnishings and fittings, plasterwork or interior decoration.[51] In addition, a vaulted ceiling would cost between £2,000 and £3,000. Total sum of the build, with furnishings and domed roof, was estimated at £26,000.[52]

The congregation was keen to begin building work on a permanent synagogue as soon as possible. The main problem with any delay was the increasing size of the congregation, as described by Benjamin Drage:

'The previous High Holy Days (1919) were attended by 330 people. For the approaching High Holy Days, we reckon on accommodating 400 people. The problem is that the place we rent (St Alban's Hall) by the kind indulgence of a Christian minister will only accommodate 300 people.'[53]

Estimates fluctuated for the build and that made it difficult to start the project without the full funds yet raised. A meeting of the committee on 4 May at Rev. Livingstone's home discussed the new estimate: £17,500 as the cost of building the first section of the synagogue, £2,000 as the estimate for furnishings, £1,300 as the cost of the freehold site, totalling £20,800. By the time the General Meeting convened on 31 May 1920, the building agreement with the Ecclesiastical Commissioners had been signed.

Communal Life

Over the summer of 1920, Lazarus Cohen was engaged as temporary reader to take Shabbat services whilst Rev. Livingstone was taking his annual holiday. A dance at the Wharncliffe Rooms raised £530, followed by a list of promises and donations, raising the sum for the Building Fund to £6,000. Sabbath and festival services continued to be held in St Alban's Hall. However, over the High Holy Days, the hall was uncomfortably overcrowded with more than 320 seats occupied. Lazarus Cohen assisted with High Holy Day services and Rev. A. A. Green gave the sermon on the 2nd day of Rosh Hashana. Mr M. Kemble and Sol Karet complained about 'the lack of decorum at services.' Other board members were quick to state that the decorum was much better than in other larger synagogues. The growth of religion classes necessitated another teacher.

Prayer for the State of Israel.

Stained glass windows were specified in the original plans.

Rev. Livingstone still struggled to arrange sufficient supplies of kosher food in the area and had yet to persuade a kosher butcher to open in Golders Green. Amidst all the hard work of pastoral and religious life, he was invited to sit on yet another committee, but one which he felt was an honour. Up and down the country, discussions were being held in towns, cities and villages about the erection of War Memorials to the fallen soldiers of the Great War. The Golders Green War Memorial Committee was duly formed, and Rev. Livingstone appointed to it. The aim of the committee was to establish a civic non-denominational memorial. Rev. Livingstone gave voice to the Jewish names that should be commemorated on it. To that end, his congregation donated the sum of £6.6.0 towards it. He and Mr J. Seaford attended the Education Conference in connection with the Jewish War Memorial.

The Literary & Social Circle still met and was extremely popular, as was the Ladies' Society under the direction of Mrs Livingstone.

The directors of the Ionic Theatre informed the

---

[51] Committee Meeting held on 26 February 1920.
[52] Committee Meeting held on 4 March 1920 at 'Aysgarth', Woodstock Road.
[53] Letter to Isidore Salmon, 16 April 1920.

congregation that it could not rent the space for High Holy Days for 1920 because it would interfere with cinema performances. High Holy Day Services reverted to St Alban's Hall, in spite of increasing numbers wishing to acquire seats for the festivals and outgrowing the available space. High Holy Day services for the autumn were assisted by Lazarus Cohen. St Alban's Hall was 'crowded to its utmost capacity, and the decorum was particularly good. 370 seats were reserved (219 men, 151 women). Dr Novis welcomed congregants to his house, and Dr. Woolf defrayed the cost of chocolates and apples for the children.'[54] The sum of £53.15s. 0d. was raised for the Jewish Board of Guardians from Rev. Livingstone's pulpit appeal.

Building Work Begins

Rough sketch plans of the synagogue were finally approved by the United Synagogue, prepared by Mr Digby Solomon for 'the first section of a permanent synagogue to be erected in Dunstan Road, Golders Green'. The synagogue was to be brick built, external facings brickwork with stone dressings. The gallery was to be of fire-resisting construction, the roof slated carried on steel trusses.[55] The eastern end of the building, where an additional section would be added at a later date, would be closed by a temporary brick wall. The ground floor was to accommodate 286 men, and the upper Ladies' Gallery to seat 171 women. Classrooms were to be built over the vestibule.

The total cost was now estimated at £29,000, after allowing for purchase and preparation of the site, legal costs, architects' & surveyors' fees, salary of Clerk of Works, and seating, and making up the road to comply with the Building Agreement. Plastering and internal decoration costs were not included in the pricing. Of these sums, Golders Green Synagogue agreed to pay £7,000, raised over recent years. The outstanding balance of £22,000 was to be provided by the United Synagogue as follows: £16,000 as a loan and subject to interest of 5 per cent. Of the balance, one half to be provided by the United Synagogue as a grant, free of interest, and the remaining half by a supplementary advance on the same terms as the £16,000.

At a meeting in May 1921, it was agreed that 'a letter be sent to the United Synagogue urging that the building of the synagogue be hurried on so that it would be ready for the High Festivals – at least in such a way as to enable us to hold services there.' On 26 May, the committee visited the site during the day to inspect it. Building work was finally underway. Reporting on the previous year, Benjamin Drage said that: 'the scattered units of the congregation

have become knit closer together,' and 'substantial progress has been made in the erection of the permanent synagogue in spite of most serious difficulties arising out of the aftermath of the war.'[56] He also summarized the position of the community: 'Starting from very humble beginnings, but inspired by a noble zeal, the Golders Green Synagogue is now an established institution with a membership of 324 adults and a revenue for the past year of £1,175.'

Discussions continued about the design and specifications of the interior. A letter was sent to the architects that 'the centre steel pillars are an obstruction which would seriously interfere with the convenience of seatholders.'[57] The number of seatholders was also still under negotiation. It was decided to accommodate seating in the new synagogue for 273 men and 184 women, a total of 457.

Digby Solomon, architect, was asked to have the roof ready and the ground floor levelled in time for the ceremony for laying the foundation stone that autumn. He replied in the affirmative, but also reported on other aspects of the build, i.e. that it was not possible to do away with the steel pillars, and the Ark and Almemar were not to exceed £700 in cost. The Board of Management decided, after lively discussions, that a pulpit was 'absolutely necessary as in the architect's plans so the women could see the preacher from the ladies gallery', but 'the feeling that an expenditure of £65 for a Chief Rabbi's seat was extravagant and might not be incurred.'[58] Agreement was reached to commission Bennett Furnishing Co. to make the seats for the synagogue from 'Austrian oak, upholstered, complete with book rests, lockers, keys and numbers at £2,360.' A maximum expenditure of £2,500 was agreed, to include the cost of the Warden's Box, choir seats and additional men's seating to bring it up to 273. The final numbers for seating was to be 282 for the men and 184 for women, i.e. a total of 466 adults. The synagogue was to have stained

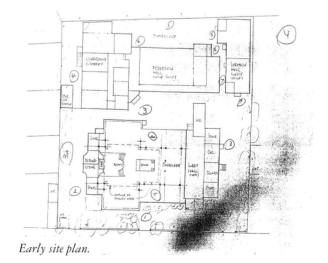

Early site plan.

---

[54] Committee Meeting held on 7 November 1921.
[55] Committee Meeting held on 19 January 1921 at 'Aysgarth', Woodstock Road.
[56] General Meeting held at St Alban's Hall, 19 June 1921.
[57] 21 July 1921.
[58] Meeting, 4 October 1921.

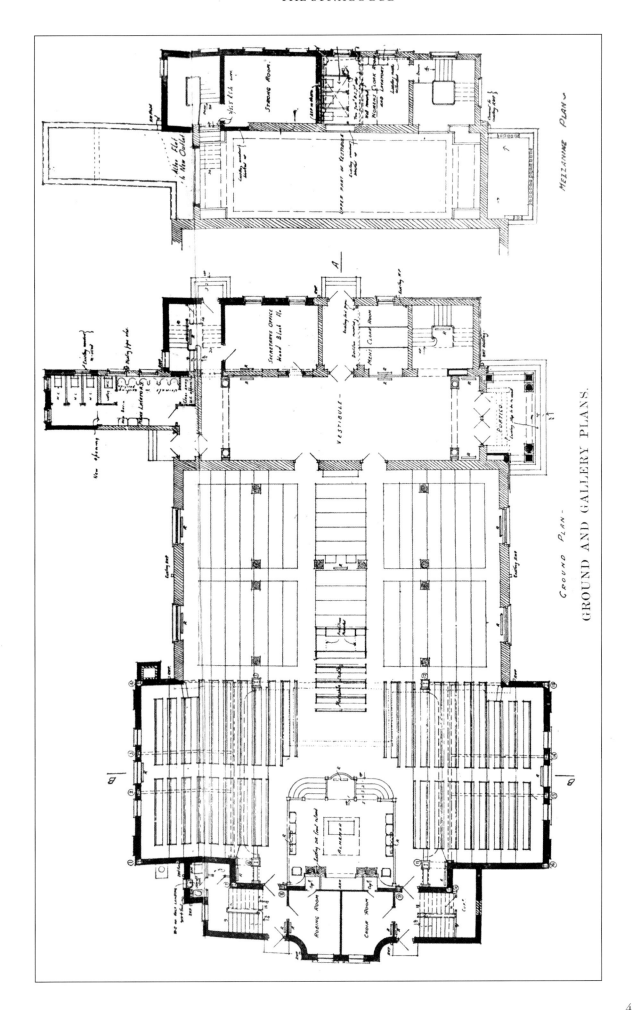

GROUND AND GALLERY PLANS.

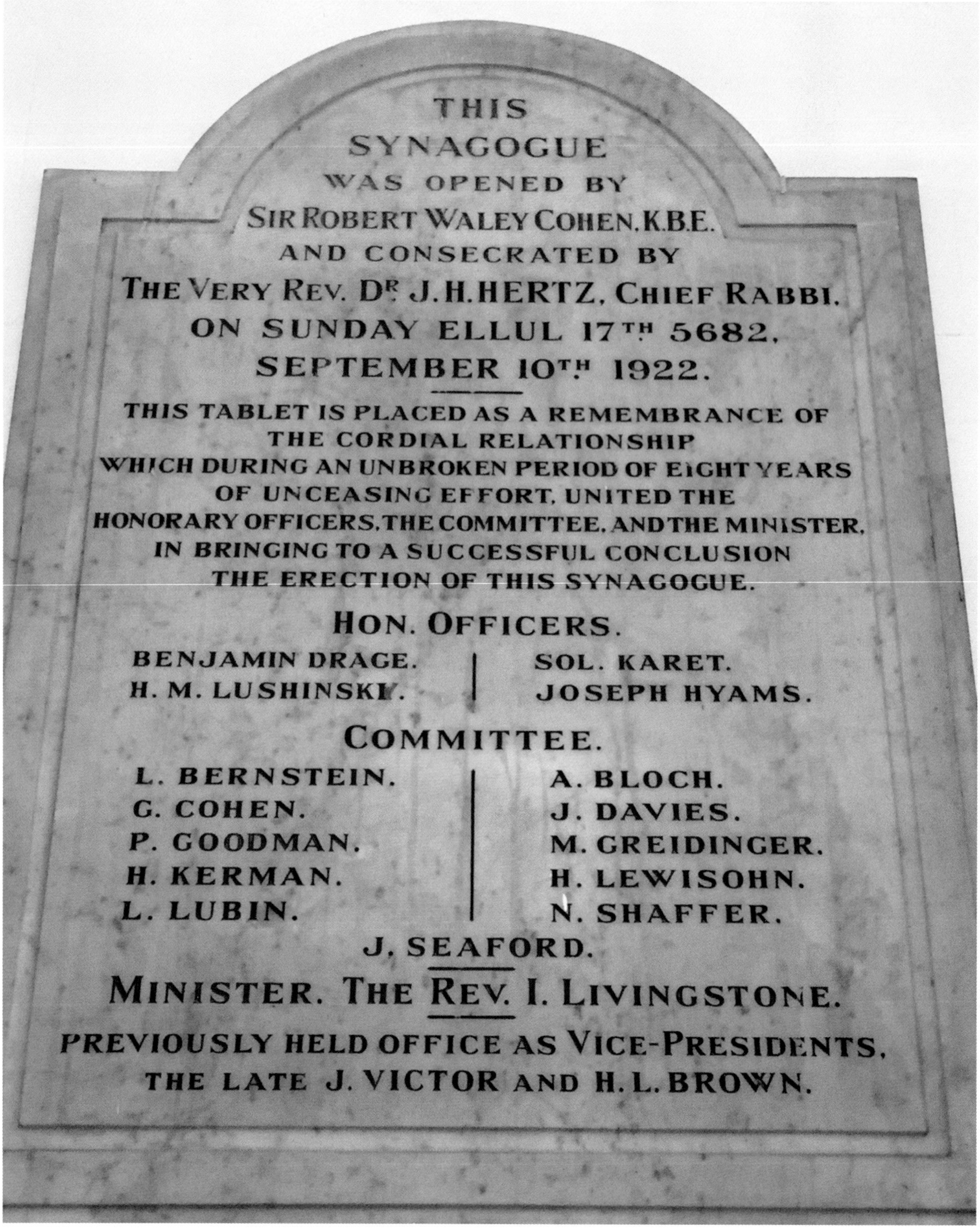

THIS
SYNAGOGUE
WAS OPENED BY
SIR ROBERT WALEY COHEN. K.B.E.
AND CONSECRATED BY
THE VERY REV. DR. J. H. HERTZ, CHIEF RABBI.
ON SUNDAY ELLUL 17TH 5682,
SEPTEMBER 10TH 1922.

THIS TABLET IS PLACED AS A REMEMBRANCE OF
THE CORDIAL RELATIONSHIP
WHICH DURING AN UNBROKEN PERIOD OF EIGHT YEARS
OF UNCEASING EFFORT, UNITED THE
HONORARY OFFICERS. THE COMMITTEE. AND THE MINISTER.
IN BRINGING TO A SUCCESSFUL CONCLUSION
THE ERECTION OF THIS SYNAGOGUE.

HON. OFFICERS.

BENJAMIN DRAGE.   SOL. KARET.
H. M. LUSHINSKY.   JOSEPH HYAMS.

COMMITTEE.

L. BERNSTEIN.   A. BLOCH.
G. COHEN.   J. DAVIES.
P. GOODMAN.   M. GREIDINGER.
H. KERMAN.   H. LEWISOHN.
L. LUBIN.   N. SHAFFER.

J. SEAFORD.

MINISTER. THE REV. I. LIVINGSTONE.

PREVIOUSLY HELD OFFICE AS VICE-PRESIDENTS,
THE LATE J. VICTOR AND H. L. BROWN.

glass windows, and as such sketches of designs for them were shown to the committee.

The Minute Book also notes: 'With the approaching completion of the erection of the synagogue, the subject of the laying of the road immediately adjacent to the synagogue, should be taken up with the Ecclesiastical Commissioners, and pointing out that if a public road was not laid, the approaches to the synagogue would be impassable during the wet season.'[59] Nancie Craig, Rev. Livingstone's eldest daughter, once recalled: 'On Shabbat we used to go to the site and see how the new building was progressing.'[60]

---

[59] Entry 4 October 1921.
[60] *Jewish Chronicle*, 12 January 1996.

On 16 October 1921, Lionel de Rothschild OBE, MP, President of the United Synagogue, laid the foundation stone. It was attended by a large assembly, including many representative communal workers. The service was conducted by Rev. Livingstone and Rev. G. Prince, the latter conducted the choral portions with the aid of the choir of St John's Wood Synagogue. A silver trowel was presented to Lionel de Rothschild. Speakers at the consecration were Chief Rabbi Dr Hertz, Lionel de Rothschild, Rev. A. A. Green of Hampstead Synagogue, Benjamin Drage and Rev. Livingstone.

By the end of the year, plans for the Ark and Almemar were approved. Work proceeded for the large stained glass window on the first floor at a cost of £39. The theme of the window was Creation. Benjamin Drage had written to the United Synagogue pointing out that a recess was 'an imperative necessity and that it would permit an extra 23 additional seats with the prospect of an extra £250 in funds.' New designs for stained glass windows were being prepared. It was agreed that the Almemar and Ark should be visible from every part of the Ladies' Gallery. There was now a waiting list for membership of the Hampstead Synagogue, so it was suggested that these people could be referred to Golders Green Synagogue for possible membership.

By 1922, membership had increased to 200 males and 150 females. Services were still being held in St Alban's Hall during the construction of the new synagogue. The first part of the year was taken up with debates about the cost of oak panelling for the synagogue, also the price quoted for the stained glass windows was deemed too expensive. Other items discussed were lighting and the cost of internal decoration of the synagogue. Finally, at a meeting in February, the architect's scheme of interior decoration was approved for oak panelling with plaster walls above. The pillars were to be encased in Austrian oak and therefore similar to the oak panelling. The United Synagogue offered to defray £925 of the cost of the interior if the synagogue contributed £400. The Entertainment Committee raised £524.00 for other equipment for the synagogue. A further issue became pressing. Because the synagogue backed onto playing fields, five windows had already been broken. Lewis Solomon & Sons were asked to add protection to the windows.

Consecration of the Synagogue

An advertisement was placed for the post of temporary second reader to start for the High Holy Days. This led to the appointment of Rev. Asher Littenberg from the Bayswater Synagogue as temporary second reader. An advertisement was also placed in Jewish newspapers for the position of Beadle, also doorkeeper and cleaner. As work continued on the final stages of the synagogue building, the

Interior of the synagogue, 1927.

43

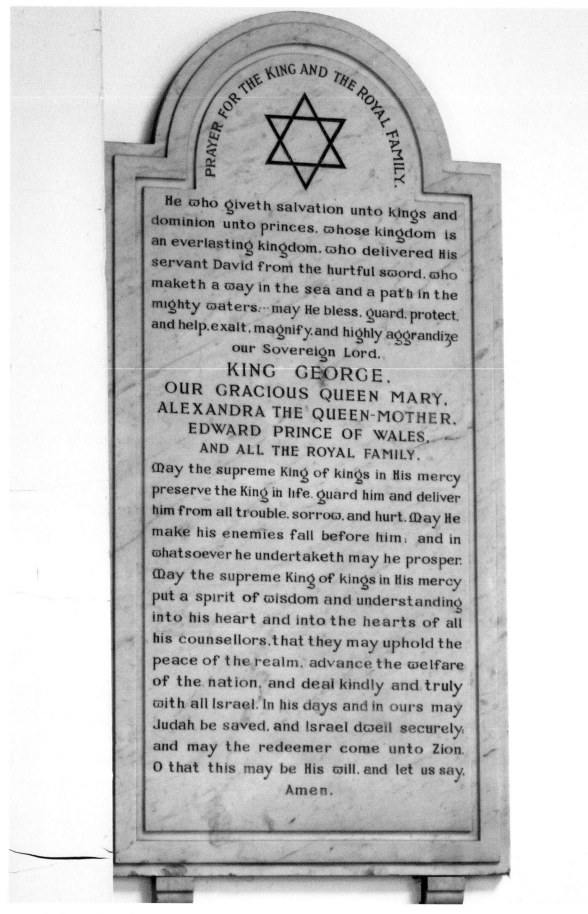

Prayer for the Royal Family.

Board of Management turned its attention to a resolution to be sent to the Council of the League of Nations that stated: 'This meeting respectfully appeals to the Council of the League of Nations to ratify the Palestine Mandate providing for Jewish National Home without further delay.'[61] It would be another 26 years before the Jewish people would see the establishment of the State of Israel.

The consecration of the synagogue took place on 10 September 1922, officiated by Chief Rabbi Dr Hertz, Sir Robert Waley Cohen. Rev. Livingstone's surviving daughter, Barbara Michaels, now in her late nineties, remembers it:

> 'It was quite an occasion and I was only young at the time. My sister and I were allowed to attend the service but had to go home to our maid afterwards. We were considered far too young to attend the reception. There was many dignitaries and proper ceremony. It was a big day for our community.'

That day, it was quite a procession that entered the synagogue to *Ma Tovu* and *Baruch Haba* by the choir of the Great Synagogue. The scroll bearers were the Chief Rabbi Sir Robert Waley Cohen, Rev. Livingstone, Dayanim S. Hillman, L. Mendelsohn, H. M. Lazarus, Rev. A. A. Green, S. Moses, J. Prag (JP), I. Salmon, W. T. Leviansky, Benjamin Drage, Sol Karet, J. Hyams and members of the committee. An account of the opening appeared in the *Jewish Chronicle* later that week:[62]

> 'Amongst those present were several members of the Metropolitan clergy and leading members of the community. A guard of honour was furnished by a detachment of the 2nd Battalion of the Jewish Lad's Brigade under the command of Lieut. E. Jacobi… The interior is decorated in the Greek style, and all walls are beautifully panelled in oak. The seating is also of oak. Above the hall, and approached by a wide stone staircase is the Ladies' Gallery, and behind this a spacious committee room. The exterior of the synagogue is of red brick with stone cornices in the Georgian style.'

Sir Robert Waley Cohen was presented with a gold key by Benjamin Drage. Afterwards, tea was served in the hall. Since the consecration, the synagogue has become fondly known as the Dunstan Road Synagogue.

Heritage Listed Status

Today, the Golders Green Synagogue is a Grade II listed building, listed by English Heritage on 21 May 2007.[63]

View of the main synagogue from the Ladies' Gallery.

The report describes it as of:

> 'Red brick with rubbed red brick quoins and window surrounds, stone dressings and Portland stone portico. Shallow hipped roofs with central circular roof lantern. Timber sashes, and some metal-framed sashes. A traditional Neo-Georgian style externally with a lavish Italianate interior. The windows have plain slightly recessed surrounds with simple stone cills on brackets and there is a continuous stone balustraded parapet. The central section of the synagogue is of three wide bays with a shallow pyramidal hipped roof; segmental-headed windows at ground floor (the apron to one of these is a stone foundation plaque of the 1927 extension), above which are round-headed, small-pane windows at first floor, all with red brick surrounds and keyblock, then a continuous stone cornice; the right bay is set back and features the prominent stone portico that has a rectangular-plan column with entasis paired with a circular column to each side, and engaged columns behind; there is a balustraded stone parapet above the cornice.'

In particular, the listing report emphasizes the interior of the main hall as being 'the most impressive part of the building, for its scale, arrangement and quality of its fittings.' It outlines the architectural features and design of the synagogue:

> 'The interior is defined by a continuous gallery on three sides, the hall wider at the east end, and

[61] Meeting held 11 July 1922.
[62] *Jewish Chronicle*, 15 Sept 1922.
[63] Reference number: 31/0/10487.

45

View of part of the Ladies' Gallery.

Seats in the Ladies' Gallery.

The vestibule.

supported by paired Doric order columns at ground floor and Ionic at first floor. The earliest range to the west has steel supports, but the 1927 eastwards extension is supported with a concrete cantilever. The walls are lined with oak panelling. The original oak bench seating (for around 1000 people) largely survives throughout the main hall. There is a continuous dentilled cornice and a triglyph frieze along the front of the gallery. The ceiling is barrel-vaulted with dentil plasterwork, and there are semi-circular clerestory windows between each bay of the ceiling on the north and south sides. The main hall is lit by a central lantern (although the plasterwork around it fell in 2006). There is an extensive collection of colourful stained glass windows, much dating from the late 1920s, featuring memorials to past members of the synagogue and biblical themed scenes... The east end houses the Ark, the main focus of the building in architectural and worship terms. This comprises a polished oak temple front featuring 6 pilasters that have Corinthian capitals and a continuous dentilled cornice, featuring Hebrew lettering in the frieze, and also in the upper level

below the cornice (Isaiah 2:3 translated as 'For out of Zion shall go forth the law and the word of the Lord from Jerusalem'). Behind the curtain are 1970s secure doors holding the Torah scrolls. The Ark is set on a raised platform reached by an elaborate polished red-veined Sienna marble wall, pair of curved steps and central pulpit, an altogether lavish feature and dating from 1926. The central Bimah was added in 1978, placed centrally in the European, orthodox tradition (instead of at the east end).'

The final part of the listing document comprises a summary of the reasons for designation of the listing which states: 'The special interest of the 1921-27 Golders Green Synagogue resides in its historic interest as the first and major synagogue in this area, which rapidly developed as one of the most significant Jewish neighbourhoods in C20 London and where its discrete traditional Neo-Georgian exterior, designed by two of the best known Jewish architects in this period, was intended to blend in with the architecture of the area; and for its particularly impressive interior, seen in the building's scale and spatial qualities as well as the quality and intactness of its fittings.'

CHAPTER 4

Ministers, Rabbis and Readers

IN ITS FIRST hundred-year history, the Golders Green Synagogue has had a total of nine ministers and Rabbis, including two part-time Rabbis during the 1990s. The congregation's records show that each one has given dedicated service, with their own vision for the community. The first minister, Rev. Nathan Levine, took up post from 2 October 1915. Born in Swislotz (Poland) in 1890, Rev. Levine came to England as a young boy. His father, Rabbi Louis Levine, was appointed Rabbi in Liverpool. As such, Nathan Levine was raised in a house of great learning and studied at the Royal Academy of Music in London before gaining a place at Jews' College where he studied under the renowned Chazan, Rev. Spero. Golders Green Synagogue was Rev. Levine's first ministerial appointment. There, he instigated Bible classes for the children after Sabbath morning services and religion classes on Sunday mornings.[64] He also formed a choir, comprising boys and girls from the religion classes. From Golders Green, Rev. Levine was appointed to the Bayswater Synagogue, then Walthamstow Synagogue. Later saw a posting to the Port Elizabeth Hebrew Congregation in South Africa. Rev. Levine was succeeded at Golders Green Synagogue by Rev. Isaac Livingstone.[65]

In 1922, Rev. Asher Littenberg was appointed as Chazan, or Cantor, of the synagogue. Born in Poland in 1876, Rev. Littenberg came to England on his own as a teenager to stay with a relative in the East End. His first job was choirboy at the Great Fieldgate Street Synagogue. From there, he obtained a position as Chazan first in Derby, then in Bradford. The minister at Bradford at the time was Ashe Lincoln. Rev. Isaac Livingstone had succeeded Rev. Lincoln as minister there. Rev. Littenberg's grandson, Tony Lytton, comments: 'Rev. Livingstone and my grandfather were together in Bradford for a few years until my grandfather moved back to London. Their paths were destined to cross again some years later.'

During the Great War, Rev. Littenberg became second Chazan at Duke's Place Synagogue, before transferring to Bayswater. In 1922, the Board of Management of the Golders Green Synagogue elected Rev. Littenberg for the vacancy of Reader (Chazan) on a salary of £400 per annum, rising by annual increments of £10 to a maximum of £500 per annum. He and his family lived at 51 Highfield

Rev. Asher Littenberg. COURTESY: TONY LYTTON

Avenue, and once again he worked alongside Rev. Livingstone. Tony Lytton comments: 'My grandfather brought to the Golders Green Synagogue the traditional tunes from Duke's Place. That's what I grew up on. He effectively brought the music to Golders Green. He was also the local *mohel* and *shochet*.'[66] At a special meeting of the Board held on Sunday 2 January 1927, and having served four years as temporary Reader, Rev. Littenberg was unanimously appointed to the post permanently. Rev. Littenberg married Clara Milly Isaacs and they had four children: Irene, Henry, Maurice and Hilda.

When Rev. Littenberg retired in 1935, his post was filled by Rev. Moise Taschlicky who was to become the longest serving Chazan of the congregation from 1935 until 1970. The Minute Book notes that he was appointed

---

[64] Meeting on 13 February 1916 at Sol Karet's house at 17 The Ridgeway.

[65] Rev. Nathan Levine is buried in the East Ham Jewish Cemetery.

[66] Rev. Littenberg died in 1966 and is buried in the Willesden Cemetery (United Synagogue).

Rev. A. LITTENBERG

Certified Mohel

:: SINCE 1907 ::

51 HIGHFIELD AVENUE

GOLDERS GREEN.

Telephone - - - - Speedwell **2455**

Rev. Moise Taschlicky.

on a temporary basis from 1935, but permanently from 31 March 1936. Throughout his long service, Rev. Taschlicky gave devoted service to the congregation and was present at all major occasions. Born in Kherson, now Ukraine, he studied at Budapest High School of Music. In 1929, he was appointed as a Chazan to the Alte Synagoge, Berlin, and later went to Vienna. After emigrating to England, he became Chazan to the growing community at Golders Green. He edited a work well known in his time called *Sabbath Afternoon Service (Tefillat Mincha Le-shabbat) and specially arranged with Traditional Melodies* for use by the children at the Golders Green Synagogue.[67]

Edna Martin remembers him well: 'Rev. Taschlicky was very musical in both liturgical and classical music. He had a wonderfully powerful and sweet tenor voice, his presence enhancing services greatly. He also had a dog and had taught it to pick up a piece of food it liked and on hearing the word 'treif' the dog would drop it and only go back to it when 'kosher' was declared. This was an entertaining item at various community gatherings.'

The last bar mitzvah that Rev. Taschlicky conducted as Chazan was that of Jeremy Manuel in 1970. After his retirement, the Board of Management conferred on him the title of 'Emeritus Reader'.

Others who served the community were Rev. Meir Finkelstein who was inaugurated as the youngest Reader in 1970 at the age of eighteen. He was followed by Rev. Chaim Abramovitz in 1975, then Rev. Michael Binstock and Rabbi David Katanka, the latter also becoming the congregation's rabbi.

Rev. Isaac Livingstone

Rev. Isaac Livingstone succeeded Rev. Levine to become the second minister of the Golders Green Synagogue after Rev. Levine had served for congregation for the first year of its foundation. Because Rev. Levine's ministry was so brief, Rev. Livingstone is often mistakenly thought of as the congregation's first Rabbi. Born in Nottingham on 4 May 1885, Rev. Isaac Livingstone grew up in Manchester. He attended Aria College in Portsmouth for his religious education and Portsmouth Grammar for secular education. At the age of about 18 years old, he came to Jews' College London. From 1907-8, he was the visiting minister to the Aldershot Jewish community, and from 1909-1916, Minister of Bradford Synagogue. During his time in Portsmouth, he met Hetty (Henrietta) Goodman; both having taught Hebrew at the Portsmouth Synagogue. They married there in 1912 and had two daughters: Nancie, born in Bradford in 1915 and Barbara, born in Golders Green in 1917. Rev. Livingstone was formally appointed to Golders Green Synagogue in July 1916, after the committee met at Aysgarth, Woodstock Road to discuss his appointment. The Minute Book records:[68]

'That having received an application from the Rev. I. Livingstone for the position of Minister and Reader of the Golders Green Synagogue, he be required to produce a medical certificate by Dr Phineas Abraham of Harley Street before his election. It was carried unanimously that, subject to the medical certificate, Livingstone be appointed Minister and Reader of the Religion Classes and secretary of the Golders Green Synagogue at a rate of £156 pa. Mr J. Ellis appointed temporary Chazan and teacher on a salary of £1 a week.'

---

[67] I am grateful to Michael Jolles for providing this information.
[68] Minute Book entry, 2 July 1915.

Rev. Isaac Livingstone. COURTESY: BARBARA MICHAELS

Rev. Chaim Abramovitz.

Starting his ministry in Golders Green from the middle of the Great War, Rev. Livingstone served the congregation with great distinction until his retirement in 1953. Under his leadership began the lengthy project to acquire land for a synagogue, something that took up a great deal of his time – as shown by the sheer volume of correspondence in the archives and number of meetings over a six-year period until the opening of the synagogue building in 1922. His daughter Barbara recalls: 'My father was a tolerant and assimilated man, a middle of the road Orthodox who saw himself as very English. He gave many talks to non-Jewish groups, which he believed was an important part of his ministry in enabling them to understand Judaism. As for us, we were brought up as English children with responsibility to the community.'

Rev. Livingstone was known, too, as a good orator. He believed in a good education for his daughters. Until the age of ten, Barbara attended St Dunstan's School, a small private school in the Finchley Road. Wessex Gardens School, a popular school for local Jewish children, became a popular choice later. Then she and her sister Nancie attended North London Collegiate, an all-girls school then located in Camden.

The congregation was at the heart of everything that Rev. Livingstone undertook. He was a member of numerous committees, including the local civic committee to establish the Golders Green War Memorial. Every year, he attended the Armistice Day service at the War Memorial. He was an active Chaplain to the Forces, a member of the Hendon Rotary Club from 1929, and Chaplain to Alderman Joseph Freedman and his wife, Councillor Rosa Freedman, during their term as Mayor and Mayoress of Barnet in 1972–3. Just how busy Rev. Livingstone and his wife were, is reflected in the words of their daughter, Barbara who recalls: 'In about 1935 or 1936, we moved to Woodstock Road. It was there that we

had a maid because my mother was always at the shul in the evenings. She worked very hard for the community, just like my father.'

In May 1938, when Rev. and Mrs Livingstone celebrated their 25th wedding anniversary, Mr H. Hyman presented them with a silver Menorah on behalf of the synagogue. On that occasion, Mr Bolsom paid tribute to Rev. Livingstone's work in the borough and outside, especially his civic and interfaith work. Paul Goodman added to that: 'Rev. Livingstone has successfully achieved a difficult task in ministering to a heterogeneous community, the members of which had varied ideas in regard to synagogue matters and communal problems.' In addition, Mr J. Greenbaum paid tribute to the work of Mrs Livingstone with the Ladies' Society.

For many years Rev. Livingstone was actively involved in Christian-Jewish relations and became chair of the Hendon & Golders Green branch of the Council of Christians and Jews. Dayan Dr Lew once wrote: 'as the Jewish representative on many non-Jewish bodies, he was held in very high esteem for his contribution to inter-faith and inter-racial understanding.'[69] His long-time friend and once warden of the shul, Alfred Woolf, once recalled of him: 'His impeccable canonicals added much to the beauty and decorum of our services,' and his sermons were delivered with 'great homiletic ability in simple language which inspired his congregation.' Under Rev. Livingstone's leadership, the congregation became 'a very English community of an Anglicised tradition'. It had its own music and tunes for services. Rev. Livingstone himself

[69] *Jewish Chronicle*, 5 October 1979.

became affectionately known in Jewish circles as 'the Bishop of Golders Green.'

The last bar mitzvah ceremony undertaken by Rev. Livingstone was that of Brian Beckman in 1954 on Rev. Livingstone's last Shabbat service as the minister. Although retired, he continued as Emeritus Minister and led an active part in the life of the community. On the occasion of his retirement, the synagogue had a full house for his final service as Rabbi. In his address, he commented that he had accompanied the congregation 'from its childhood to its present status,' and his ministry had been a happy one. 'Those who lay the foundations of the synagogue were gifted with judgment and understanding,' he said. 'They were willing workers for the congregation's wellbeing and deserved to be remembered for good.'[70] He also paid tribute to the exceptional hard work of his wife. Afterwards, the congregation provided a luncheon in the Joseph Freedman Hall in the presence of the Board of Management and representatives of the United Synagogue. He was succeeded by Rabbi Eugene Newman.

Then in 1975, he was honoured to be elected Emeritus Minister of the United Synagogue. Amongst the many roles he undertook were the chairmanship of the Jewish Lecture Committee, the Jewish representative on the British Churches Housing Trust and the National & London Council of Social Service.

On his 94th birthday in 1979, Rev. Livingstone was given the honour of delivering a sermon from the pulpit. He died in September 1979 at the age of 94. The funeral was conducted in the synagogue by the then Chief Rabbi, Dr Immanuel Jakobovits, and the then incumbent Rabbi Dr Jonathan Sacks. Rabbi Sacks began his powerful eulogy by saying that Rev. Livingstone's death was a shock to everyone 'because we all thought he was immortal' such was his influence and presence within the community. Rev. Livingstone is buried in the Willesden Jewish cemetery, together with his wife, Hetty who died in 1981 at the age of 97.

Rabbi Eugene Newman

Rabbi Eugene Newman was born in 1913 in Bilke, a small market town in sub Carpathian Ruthenia, then in Austro-Hungary, now Ukraine. He was the sixth child of eight siblings. Two brothers and two sisters, and all their children, later perished in the Holocaust.[71] The family was strictly orthodox but not particularly Hasidic. His father was a textile merchant who opened a general store when he returned from America in 1921 where he had been trapped during the Great War. Rabbi Newman's son, Rabbi Michael Newman, says:

Rabbi Eugene Newman with Chief Rabbi Immanuel Jakobovits.

---

[70] *Hendon Times*, 5 February 1954.
[71] His surviving brothers lived in Israel after 1948.

'My father's day began when he clambered through the window into the snow so as not to disturb his parents at 3:30 a.m. to go to *Cheder*. He studied in yeshivot in Tirnau and Pressbourg, Bratislava, where he was the youngest student. Every Thursday he studied through the night there with the Rebbe's son. He was proud that he went to a German-speaking Gymnasium from where he matriculated.'

Later, he attended Prague University to read Semitics and Jewish history, as well as concurrently studying at the Rabbinical Seminary of Prague. His studies were cut short when the Nazi regime overran Czechoslovakia. He had to flee for his life, making a long and hazardous journey from Prague, as his son Winston recalls:

'My father had to hide under the seats of the last train out of the country, while German soldiers were sitting all around. He tried to get into England, but at first he was not permitted entry and was sent back to Belgium. Eventually, six weeks later, he managed to gain entry when a group of Czech students were vouched for by aristocratic well-wishers. Without any contacts or resources, and without speaking the language, he made his way to Manchester where he quickly learned English.'

Rabbi Newman served as Rabbi of New Synagogue, Manchester from 1939 until 1945. During his time in Manchester, he gained an MA degree from the university with his work on 'Jewish Medieval Views on Revelation'. It was there that he met and married Bertha Cohen in 1944, a Hebrew teacher whose family was steeped in communal service, and who hailed from a long line of Rabbis. She was a great-granddaughter of Dayan Jacob Reinovits and a granddaughter of Dayan Susman Cohen.

From Manchester, Rabbi Newman became the minister of the Portsmouth & Southsea Hebrew Congregation from 1945 to 1954. There, he acted as advisor to the Royal Navy on matters relating to Jewish servicemen, and chaplain to the local air training corps units and prisoner-of-war camps. He also visited Jewish prisoners at Parkhurst Prison on the Isle of Wight. During his time in Portsmouth, he travelled weekly to London to study at Jews' College, from where he gained his *semicha* in 1950. A learned man, he spoke a number of languages fluently: Hebrew, German, Yiddish and Czech, and had a working knowledge of several other languages including Russian, French, Hungarian, Arabic and Latin.

Moving to Dunstan Road Synagogue in 1954 was the fulfilment of Rabbi Newman's dream to serve a large and vibrant Jewish community. He and his wife threw themselves into service of this community with total dedication. Rabbi Michael Newman recalls his father's qualities as Rabbi: 'He had a very good memory for names and faces. He was a kindly man of great presence, a scholar and teacher, a true friend, good listener and wise counsellor. He was a man of peace who worked hard to avoid

confrontation or broiges and often mediated in disputes within families. He respected his wardens and maintained good relations with them all. He layned on a regular basis several times a month, which was unusual, as most rabbis at the time did not layn at all.'

Rabbi Newman worked tirelessly for the congregation, especially with the youth and started a study circle for teenagers, which met on Shabbat afternoons in the shul in the summer. During the winter, for many years, it met on Friday nights at his home in Wycombe Gardens. He introduced and encouraged monthly youth services, which the youth conducted themselves, and encouraged the children's services. He was appointed member of the Youth Sub-Committee of the Hendon Education Committee. He also instituted his regular Talmud Shiur on Shabbat afternoons after *Mincha*, which was attended by distinguished members, including Ashe Lincoln QC, and held regular classes in modern Hebrew. Many congregants remember that he instigated a special prayer for Israel's defence forces after the prayer for Israel during the Shabbat service. Bertha Newman was also involved in all aspects of the life of the synagogue, supporting her husband's ministry. 'She was especially instrumental in initiating and implementing the provision of a Kosher School meals service for Jewish children in local non-Jewish schools,' recalls their daughter Adele. She adds:

'The meals were held in the Joseph Freedman Hall. It was a major undertaking and she was involved in organising the coach rotas to transport the children to and from school, with other mothers supervising. Even today those who attended remember it with affection as being an important part of their formative Jewish experience. She also had her own charitable endeavours and supported my father. I remember my father as a conscientious man who made frequent pastoral visits to members of the community. On Purim, he would read the *megilla* to several elderly members in their own homes.'

Rabbi Newman protesting at treatment of Russian Jews in a demonstration outside Russian Embassy, London, 1960s.
COURTESY: THE NEWMAN FAMILY

For some years, Rabbi Newman was a member of Chief Rabbi Jakobovits' cabinet, with the portfolio for welfare. He was active nationally, too, in the public campaign for Soviet Jewry. Well before this campaign, he regularly raised the plight of Soviet Jewry in his sermons. He was active in the men's Mizrachi movement and a great spokesman for Israel. Amongst his pastoral duties, he undertook to be the Jewish chaplain to New End Hospital and Athlone House Convalescent Home, visiting them on a weekly basis. Always a strong advocate of Jewish schools, he helped to establish Mathilda Marks Kennedy School at Barclay House, Golders Green which started in 1958 under the auspices of the Zionist Federation. He became their honorary principal. A number of publications came out over the years. His major scholarly work was on the Shelah Hakadosh, the foremost Chief Rabbi in early seventeenth century Europe. This was researched for his Ph.D thesis, conferred in 1968 from London University, and later published as a book in 1972 as *Life and Teachings of Isaiah Horovitz*.[72]

During 1967, Dayan Morris Swift moved into the Golders Green area. The congregation suggested that he be given a corner seat in the shul 'formerly occupied by the late Rev. Littenberg' and that it 'be suitably adapted, similar to the one Rev. Livingstone occupies.'[73] Dayan Swift aided Rabbi Newman, and his presence in the congregation would be a blessing at one of the saddest moments in the community's history because on Shabbat Vayigash 1st Jan 1977, Rabbi Newman died suddenly at home as he was preparing to go to the Shabbat service in the synagogue. He was 63 years old and had served the congregation for twenty-three years. Alan Mays remembers that fateful day:

'He collapsed just before the Shabbat morning service. Someone sent for a doctor from the shul. It was not until the end of the morning service that the cantor said to Dayan Swift: 'The Rabbi's gone.' Dayan Swift asked: 'What do you mean?' Nothing further was said to the congregation at that point. In his sermon, Dayan Swift mentioned "a rose being plucked from our midst". No one saw the significance of his comment until the end of the service when the announcement was made. It left everyone in great shock. The subsequent funeral, with the coffin in the synagogue, made for solemn and dignified prayers. The shul was completely packed with mourners, including local Hassidim. Rabbi Newman had a huge send-off that Sunday morning.'

Jackie Crossley, a long-standing member of the shul and its current vice-chair, also expressed the loss felt by the congregation: 'I for one will never forget the feeling of

sadness and loss that permeated the shul on that day. He was a great influence during my youth, and through him I gained a love and involvement in all aspects of shul life.'

During his time as Rabbi at Golders Green, Rabbi Newman had tried to instigate a central *bimah* in the synagogue, but it had not met with approval. Rabbi Michael Newman comments: 'The idea of a central bimah was to try to attract some more orthodox members. However, the shul did not support him in this matter, and he felt that it had lost the opportunity to attract members. It was not until after my father passed away that the shul thought it appropriate to erect a new central *bimah* in his memory.' The bimah, which was designed by his son and architect Winston Newman, stood from 1978 to 2014.'

Rabbi Newman was, in the words of one congregant: 'a deeply committed communal Rabbi, a true servant of the community.'[74]

Dayan Morris Swift

After the sudden death of Rabbi Newman, Dayan Morris Swift agreed to become the acting minister during the interregnum. Only six months after retiring from the Beth Din, he was recalled to full time service at Golders Green while the process began to find a new full time minister. Born in Liverpool in 1907, he went on to have a distinguished career in the Anglo-Jewish community. Dayan Swift had studied for several years at the Mir Yeshiva in Poland, and later served as a rabbi in Los Angeles, and a member of the Beth Din (Rabbinical Court) in Johannesburg, South Africa. From 1957-76, he became a full time member of the London Beth Din. He would serve the Golders Green Synagogue twice as temporary minister,

Dayan Swift. COURTESY: TERRY SOPEL

[72] In 1951, Rabbi Newman wrote *Facts about the Portsmouth Jewish Community* which was quoted by Anglo-Jewish historian, Cecil Roth.
[73] Entry in the Minute Book, 23 May 1967.
[74] Alan Mays, interview with the author, February 2015.

something which he carried out 'with undiminished vigour. A charismatic and very orthodox man.'[75] Dayan Swift was well known for his strict interpretation of Halacha or Jewish Law. Daniel Greenberg, who grew up in the community in the 1970s, recalls him as:

'A towering personality. His occasional *droshos* [expositions], even before he became the acting Rabbi, were a major entertainment; and he deliberately affected a flamboyance that would please the audience. We enjoyed the overdone *Stop the World, I Want to Get Off* rhetoric, and I certainly never doubted that it conveyed a serious and sincere passion and commitment to authentic Judaism.'

During his first temporary period as minister, a number of candidates applied for the post, but the congregation appointed a young and then relatively unknown, Rabbi Dr Jonathan Sacks.[76]

Dayan Swift died in September 1983 at the age of 76, and only a week after handing over the pulpit to the synagogue's new full-time Rabbi. A special Memorial Service was held in the Golders Green Synagogue at 6 p.m on 9 October 1983. Officiants were Chief Rabbi Jakobovits, Dayan I. Berger, Rabbi Ivan Binstock, Rev. Chaim Abramovitz and Rev. Michael Binstock.

Rabbi Jonathan Sacks

Jonathan Sacks took up post as the Rabbi of Golders Green Synagogue from 1 September 1978 until 1982. Inducted at the synagogue on 12 September, he was a great leader, philosopher and scholar. Born in London in 1948, Rabbi Sacks was educated at St Mary's Primary School, then Christ's College Finchley. He attended Gonville and Caius College, Cambridge, and gained a first-class Honours Degree in Philosophy. While a student there, he travelled to New York to meet Rabbi Menachem Schneerson, the Lubavitcher Rebbe, who urged him to train for the Rabbinate. He continued his studies at New College, Oxford, and King's College London, where he completed his doctorate in 1981. That same year, he was ordained at Jews' College and Yeshiva Etz Chaim, both in London. In 1970, he had married his wife, Elaine, and they have three children, Joshua, Dina and Gila and several grandchildren.

Golders Green was Rabbi Sacks' first rabbinic appointment. He came with a vision to carry the community forward by establishing a vibrant and active adult education programme, discussed in more detail in another chapter of the book.

From 1983 until 1990, Rabbi Sacks became the Rabbi of Marble Arch Synagogue in central London. During his time there, from 1984 until 1990, he served also as Principal of Jews' College. From 1 September 1991, he

Rabbi Dr Jonathan Sacks.

succeeded Lord Jacobovits as Chief Rabbi of the United Hebrew Congregations of Great Britain and the Commonwealth. Serving this position until 1 September 2013, he became an internationally recognised public figure who did much to explain the tenets of Jewish faith and tradition to the non-Jewish world. Passionate about the importance of inter-faith cooperation, he was active in inter-faith relations on many levels, something for which he was honoured with a Knighthood in the Queen's Birthday Honours in 2005, 'for services to the Community and to Inter-faith Relations'. The following September of 2006, he was made an Honorary Freeman of the London Borough of Barnet.

In 2009, Rabbi Sacks was honoured with a peerage and became Baron Sacks of Aldgate in the City of London. To this distinguished career can be added numerous visiting professorships in Britain, Israel and the United States, and also sixteen honorary degrees, one of which was a Doctorate of Divinity conferred on him by Lord Carey, a former Archbishop of Canterbury. Lord Sacks contributes widely in the national media, having appeared frequently on BBC Radio 4's Thought for the Day, or writing opinion columns in the Times. He was invited to represent the Jewish community at the wedding of Prince William and Kate Middleton. In May 2013 to mark the completion of his time as Chief Rabbi, a Gala Dinner was held in his honour at which HRH The Prince of Wales called him a 'light unto this nation' whose 'guidance on any given issue has never failed to be of practical value and deeply grounded in the kind of wisdom that is increasingly hard to come by.'

Lord Sacks has written over 25 books, including *Crisis and Covenant, Will We Have Jewish Grandchildren? Arguments for the Sake of Heaven*, and *The Dignity of Difference*. His latest

---

[75] Fifty-Fifth Annual Report, 1977–8.
[76] Amongst those who applied was Rabbi Bernard Susser whose father, Mendel, served as beadle at Golders Green for over twenty years.

54

is entitled *Not in God's Name: Confronting Religious Violence.* He has received widespread acclaim as a great thinker, broadcaster and teacher. In addition to his international travelling, public engagements and prolific writing, Lord Sacks has served as the *Ingeborg and Ira Rennert Global Distinguished Professor of Judaic Thought* at New York University and *Professor of Law, Ethics and the Bible* at King's College London. He remains a member of Golders Green Synagogue.

Dayan Ivan Binstock

Ivan Binstock grew up in Hackney and studied at Hackney Downs School and Etz Chaim Yeshiva. He graduated with a degree in Chemistry from University College London, where he continued to do post-graduate research whilst also studying under Rabbi Nachum Rabinovitch at Jews' College. He had been a Reader of the South East London Synagogue and the minister of the Finsbury Park Synagogue and New Synagogue. After marrying Rachie Werjuka, they went to Israel where he continued his studies at Mir Yeshiva in Jerusalem. He was appointed Rabbi of Golders Green Synagogue in 1983 and served until 1996. Brian Beckman comments: 'He was a good communal Rabbi, a good speaker and scholar.'

In 1989, Rabbi Binstock was invited to join the London Beth Din where he continues to serve as a Dayan. Since 1996, Dayan Binstock has been the Rabbi of St John's Wood Synagogue. Amongst his duties are pastoral counselling and adult education. He is a popular speaker in the wider community and also actively engaged in inter-faith relations as a founding member of the inter-faith organisation Pathways and the Council of Imams and Rabbis. He is the Principal of North West London Jewish Day School and the Rabbinical Advisor to Immanuel College. He is the editor of the Minhag Anglia version of

Dayan Ivan Binstock.

the Koren Mahzor for the festivals and High Holidays. He and Rachie have eight children, and a number of grandchildren.

Rabbi David Katanka.
COURTESY: THE KATANKA FAMILY

Rabbi David Katanka

After Dayan Binstock came Rabbi David Katanka, who was originally appointed Chazan of the Golders Green Synagogue. Born in December 1950, he was the son of cantor, Rev. Morris Katanka. He studied at Liverpool Yeshiva and at Jews' College, London, where he obtained his *chazanut* diploma with distinction. He undertook Rabbinical ordination to become a fully-qualified rabbi after studying at Manchester Kollel in 1990. He was also a qualified mohel, and held an MA degree in Hebrew and Jewish Studies from London University. He studied voice production with John Hargreaves, vocal consultant with the English National Opera, and served as Honorary Secretary of the Association of Chazanim of Great Britain. From 1970-72, he served the congregation at Chiswick, then Bayswater & Maida Vale (1972-1975), Brixton (1975-1978), Moortown Synagogue, Leeds (1978-1985), Sheffield (1985-1990), and Golders Green Synagogue from 1990 until 2000.

Rabbi Katanka took on the role at Golders Green at a difficult time in the congregation's life, when decline had set in, and kept the community going. 'He had the most beautiful voice,' recalls one congregant. For a while, he was aided by Rabbi Djanogly and together they shared the religious and pastoral duties. After Golders Green, he moved to the Edinburgh community from 2000 until 2003, Portsmouth from 2004–2011 and St Annes from 2013 until 2014. He passed away on 10 February 2014.

Rabbi Dr Harvey Belovski

The present incumbent of the congregation is Rabbi Belovski who arrived in the post on 1 April 2003. Described by one congregant as 'a man of enormous energy,' he was born in London, and graduated with an Honours degree in Maths from the University of Oxford. He has been married to Vicki for 26 years, whom he met at Oxford. They married in 1989 and have seven children. Having left Oxford in 1989, Rabbi Belovski and his wife moved to Gateshead where he studied at Gateshead Yeshiva and Beis HaTalmud Kollel until 1997. Having received his ordination, he became Rabbi of Loughton and Chigwell Synagogue in Essex. From there, he became Rabbi at Ilford Federation Synagogue in 2000. In 2003, he was appointed Rabbi of Golders Green Synagogue. In 2011, he completed a Ph.D in Hermeneutics at London University to become the third Rabbi of the congregation with a doctorate. His wife, Rebbetzin Vicki, active also in the community, is a freelance journalist and editor of an Orthodox newspaper.

In 2013, Rabbi Belovski was invited to participate in two major interfaith events: one at Westminster Abbey and the other a debate in the Westminster Faith Debate series. He has also instigated the site of the shul as the new blood donation centre after the Hindu Temple, once located on the corner of Helenslea Avenue and Finchley Road to Kingsbury, was no longer functioning there.

Rabbi Belovski is serving the congregation at an exciting time of revival. Part of his vision and philosophy is to encourage freshness of ideas, creativity and congregant participation. The relationship is not one-way, as Rabbi Belovksi comments:

'The shul has enabled me to grow as a Rabbi and supported my belief in Rabbinic diversification. When the Rabbi is able to undertake a number of different aspects in his life, including some outside pursuits and studies, he brings a creative dynamism which benefits the congregation and generates a flow of new ideas which helps a thriving community to continue the journey.'

Rabbi Dr Harvey Belovski.

It is a full life which Rabbi Belovski leads, aided recently by the appointment of a new assistant rabbi and rebbetzin couple, Rabbi Sam and Hadassah Fromson.

In recent years, Rabbi Belovski has gained an MSc in Organisational Psychology and trained as a coach; all skills which aid his pastoral work. He is the Rabbi for the University Jewish Chaplaincy, Head of Modern Jewish Thought at the London School of Jewish Studies, Principal of Rimon Jewish School, and also Rabbi of Kisharon, an organisation that supports children and adults with special needs.

Rabbi Belovski spends time mentoring rabbis, running seminars for rabbis, contributes regularly to *Pause for Thought* on BBC radio, and has a high inter-faith profile. 'It is important to have a varied career,' he says, 'because that makes for a better Rabbi.'

CHAPTER 5

The Inter-War Years

Golders Green Underground station 1920s, with the war memorial seen left. COURTESY: HENDON LIBRARY & ARCHIVES

DURING THE 1920s and 30s, the main thoroughfare of the Golders Green Road became a vibrant place. And yet against this backdrop, the tragedy and scars of the Great War were visible in the wounded ex-soldiers begging on the streets or selling matches. 'They were soldiers who had returned from war to find high unemployment and economic hardship for them and their families,' recalls Barbara Michaels. The president of the synagogue, Benjamin Drage, acknowledged that: 'the building of the synagogue had been accomplished during the most trying period of the war and its aftermath.'[77]

Up and down the country, committees were formed to establish war memorials to the fallen soldiers of the Great War. So too, Golders Green. In the early 1920s, Rev. Livingstone was appointed to the local committee alongside other religious leaders to investigate what should be erected by way of a War Memorial and the names to be included. Today, the iconic clock tower War Memorial is

probably the single most recognisable landmark in Golders Green, with perhaps the exception of the old BBC Hippodrome.

By now, the need for a kosher butcher in Golders Green had become a pressing concern. It was a battle that Rev. Livingstone was still fighting as the congregation entered its first year in the new building. He had already liaised with Messrs. F. Barnett & Co who were based in Middlesex Street in the East End, and their correspondence survives in the synagogue archives.[78] Two years earlier, Rev. Livingstone had tried to argue, at the very least, for Barnett & Co to supply kosher meat to local Jewish residents as part of his wider delivery schedules. In an attempt to convince Barnett & Co that it was a viable business option, Rev. Livingstone sent Barnett & Co a list of synagogue members who would be guaranteed customers and added: 'I am anxiously hoping to see the immediate establishment of a kosher butcher shop in Golders Green, or failing that,

---

[77] Comment made at the General Meeting on 6 May 1923.

[78] Golders Green Synagogue has an extensive archive of papers, correspondence and records dating back to its foundation in 1915, which make for fascinating reading.

the provision of facilities to purchase kosher meat at a local non-Jewish shop.'[79] During 1922, he turned his attention to another kosher butcher. Writing on 19 January 1922 to J. Nathan Ltd, kosher butcher and poulterer of 105 High Road, Kilburn, he said:

> 'I am happy to know that, by your keen enterprise, you have established premises at 22 North End Road for the sale of kosher meat and delicatessen. Facilities for obtaining kosher meat have long been needed in this district, and the absence of these facilities has possibly increased the neglect of the valuable dietary laws of our faith. I am anxious to do all I can to prevent any drift from Jewish observance and practice, and for this reason in particular I am glad that you have opened a branch in Golders Green.'

The 1920s and 30s was a period of formality where wardens donned top hats and the ladies wore fashionable hats. The congregation settled into the new building and numerous societies flourished, including The Literary & Social Circle and the Ladies' Society, the latter very active in charitable work. Golders Green Jewish Circle, which was affiliated to

the Union of Jewish Literary Societies, met regularly, having elected Rev. Livingstone as its president, Mr. H. G. Kay as treasurer and Miss Irene Kay as Hon. Secretary. On High Holy Days, there was standing room only and overflow services arranged. For at least the next five decades, the synagogue would be bursting to capacity on High Holy Days. Hebrew classes for the children were given by Mr Orla, Miss Scheer and Rev. Livingstone on Sunday mornings from 10am until noon. By 1924–5, the *cheder* had grown to 81 pupils on the roll.

During the decade of the 1920s, the Board of Management took a small but unprecedented step and voted to 'confer upon women the same voting powers as now enjoyed by male seatholders.'[80] The vote was proposed by Sol Karet and passed unanimously. However it would be at least another 70 years or so before women were able to be elected to the Board and 80 years before they could hold positions of management.

Communal Life

By July 1922, it became clear that the synagogue should advertise for the post of temporary Second Reader for the High Holy Days. At a meeting on 11 July 1922, it was agreed to appoint Rev. Asher Littenberg from the Bayswater Synagogue.[81] 'My father and Rev. Littenberg walked to shul together every Shabbat. They were great friends,' says Barbara Michaels. An advertisement was also placed for the positions of Beadle, door-keeper and cleaner.

The synagogue was also preoccupied with events happening outside the narrow confines of Golders Green and on 11 July 1922, the Board of Management agreed to send a resolution to the Council of the League of Nations as follows: 'that this meeting respectfully appeals to the Council of the League of Nations to ratify the Palestine Mandate providing for Jewish National Home without further delay.'[82]

The Minute Book makes a specific point of noting that on 2 November, the Board met for the first time in the synagogue's new Committee Room.

The following May 1923, the congregation officially approved the appointment of Rev. Livingstone as its permanent Minister, Reader and Secretary on a salary of £590 per annum,[83] but it also becomes apparent from the Minute Books that the congregation still needed to raise funds to pay off some of the debt for the original work of the synagogue's interior.

An entry in the Minute Book also records a letter from Buckingham Palace dated 30 November 1925 in which 'The private Secretary is commanded by their Majesties the King and Queen to thank the seatholders and members of

[79] Letter dated 3 September 1920 in the synagogue archives.
[80] Passed on 3 May 1925.
[81] Rev. Littenberg moved into a house at 51 Highfield Avenue.
[82] Minute Book entry, 11 July 1922.
[83] General Meeting held on 6 May 1923.

Wedding of Alfred Woolf to Daisy Wollman, 31 January 1923.

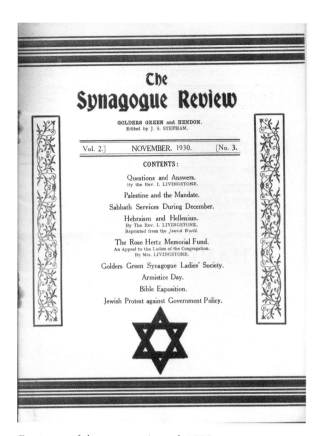

Front cover of the synagogue journal, 1930.

Expansion of the Synagogue Building

Perhaps one of the most extraordinary issues faced by the Board of Management is that during the planning and building stages of the initial synagogue, the Board knew that the community would outgrow the physical building almost immediately. Working through the documentation, it is not clear why the congregation did not build a larger synagogue at the very outset. The main reason appears to be due to finances, but also the desire not to delay having a purpose-built synagogue because the community was expanding and desperately needed its own place of worship. By 1926, the community could not wait any longer to raise the extra funds for a larger synagogue. The community had relied heavily on the United Synagogue for financial support, and the United Synagogue was unwilling to authorise extra funds beyond what had already been agreed.

By the end of 1924, synagogue membership consisted of 271 males and 200 women. Within two years of the consecration of the synagogue, the Board of Management began to plan for an extension to the synagogue to double the seating capacity for services. By 1926, there were simply not enough seats for High Holy Day Services, and the community had to hire St Alban's Hall where it had originally worshipped from 1915 until 1922, for overflow services.[84] Mr. Goldston was appointed Reader for the overflow services at a fee of 20 guineas.

Discussions began on an extension to the synagogue that included the appointment of Ernest Joseph as architect. Ernst M. Joseph was a leading designer of synagogues, having been engaged on the Art Deco synagogue at Sheepcote Street in Birmingham, and famously the St. John's Wood Liberal Synagogue in London. Plans were drawn up and approved by the Board of Management for extension work to the Golders Green Synagogue, estimated at £25,000. The wall of the eastern end of the synagogue, containing the Ark, was to be pulled down and self-supporting arches as part of the structure. It was noted that there would be 'no columns in the new section so there is a clear view from the Ladies' Gallery of the Ark and Almemar, making it 15 ft wider.' The increased seating would accommodate an extra 300 men to bring it to a total of 606 male worshippers, and an extra 176 seats for women, bringing the total of female worshippers to a total of 388. Plans also included the erection of a classroom block in the grounds, approx. 60ft by 30ft in size and to be divided into five classrooms, an extended vestibule in the shul and a pillared portico at the front of the synagogue.

On 6 September 1926, the Board examined and approved plans for the extension to the synagogue with the following additions: windows to have metal frames instead of wooden ones, the warden's box to have a bow front and doors at each side as well as in the centre, keystones to be

Golders Green Synagogue for their message of sympathy on the death of her Majesty Queen Alexandra.' The original Prayer for the Royal Family still hangs in the synagogue today, to the left of the Ark, and refers to King George V and Queen Mary.

Always conscious of its duty towards charitable causes, the congregation was extremely active in raising money for good causes throughout its hundred-year history. During the inter-war years, it raised substantial sums of money annually, for example, for the Orphan Aid Society. The president of the Charity Committee at this time was Mr M. Stephany. The vice-presidents were Rev. Livingstone, Mr L. Hyams and Mr J. Phillips, treasurer Mr C. Langdon, Hon Secretary Mrs E. Ascher and Assistant Hon. Sec. Mr M. Jacobs. Funds were raised for the Jewish National Movement which supported Jewish revival in Palestine. The Ladies' Society run by Mrs Livingstone and aided by Mrs H. Lewisohn, Mrs R. Geneen and Mrs G. Cohen, often provided support in numerous ways to the life of the synagogue and religion classes. The society met once a fortnight and made garments for various charities and institutions, such as the Stepney After-Care Committee, the Jewish Home of Rest, and the Jewish Maternity Home. The Literary and Social Society was still active in this period, run by Rev. Livingstone, J. Hyams, J. Somper JP, J. Rosenthal, Dr L. S. Woolf and Mrs S. Josephs (Hon. Sec).

---

[84] Minute Book entry, 13 July 1926.

New portico of the synagogue, 1927.

placed in the arches of the windows, the Ark to be semi-circular and of a more commanding appearance, provision to be made for a side pulpit, and a sum set aside for the future redecoration of the building. It was proposed that the new classrooms be named The Benjamin Drage Hall in 'consideration of the great services rendered by him.' The Board sought to engage Drage's approval of the idea, but Drage decided that he did not want a building in his name. The United Synagogue also notified the community that it could not name a building after someone still alive.[85]

Decorum was still an issue such that Chief Rabbi Dr Hertz told Rev. Livingstone that he had heard from two or three sources that 'unseemly and indecorous behaviour occurred in the synagogue during the recent High Festivals.' Such comments appear periodically in Minute Books of the congregation. At this time, the choir was led by Mr B. Busky who had made improvements to the efficiency of the choir. Appeals continued for donations for

the expansion of the synagogue. The United Synagogue had agreed to provide £25,000 if the synagogue could raise £1,500. Various fund-raising activities were undertaken, including a concert in the London Pavilion on 17 October 1926.

Extension work to the synagogue actually commenced in early 1927 and was expected to be completed within nine months. It would be twice the size of the original synagogue to become one of the largest Jewish places of worship in the country at that time, seating around a thousand people. During the building work, daily morning services were still held.

On 8 May 1927, the new spacious classrooms at the rear of the shul were opened by Sir Robert Waley Cohen, KBE,[86] and consecrated by Chief Rabbi Dr J. H. Hertz. The number of children enrolled in the *cheder* had risen from 80 to 120. The Classroom Committee consisted of Rev. Livingstone (Hon. Superintendent), Messrs P. Goodman, J. Greenbaum, J. Seaford, A. Jacobs, A. W. Woolf and L. Bernstein. The new classrooms with their characteristic large windows admitted plenty of natural light and became the focal point for generations of children who would receive their religious education there. The classrooms were used, too, for the regular meetings of the Jewish Lads' Brigade that met under the charge of Lieut. Sidney Grant.

Consecration of the Extended Synagogue

Sir Robert Waley Cohen and Chief Rabbi Dr J. H. Hertz reopened the newly extended synagogue in a Consecration Service on Sunday 18 September 1927. Sir Robert Waley

Consecration of the synagogue after its extension, 1927.

[85] That was United Synagogue ruling then, but today it is possible to name something after a living person.
[86] The then Vice-chairman of the United Synagogue.

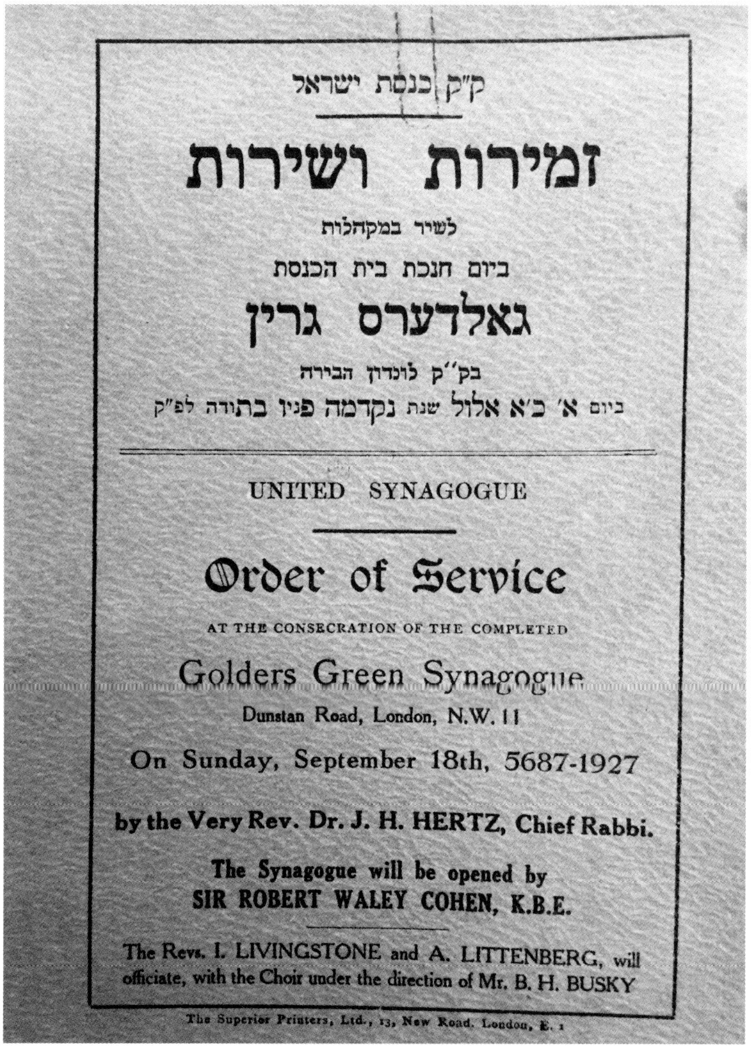

ק״ק כנסת ישראל

זמירות ושירות

לשיר במקהלות

ביום חנכת בית הכנסת

גאלדערס גרין

בק״ק לונדון הבירה

ביום א׳ כ״א אלול שנת נקדמה פניו בתודה לפ״ק

UNITED SYNAGOGUE

Order of Service

AT THE CONSECRATION OF THE COMPLETED

Golders Green Synagogue

Dunstan Road, London, N.W. 11

On Sunday, September 18th, 5687-1927

by the Very Rev. Dr. J. H. HERTZ, Chief Rabbi.

The Synagogue will be opened by
SIR ROBERT WALEY COHEN, K.B.E.

The Revs. I. LIVINGSTONE and A. LITTENBERG, will
officiate, with the Choir under the direction of Mr. B. H. BUSKY

The Superior Printers, Ltd., 13, New Road, London, E. 1

Consecration programme for the synagogue service, 1927.

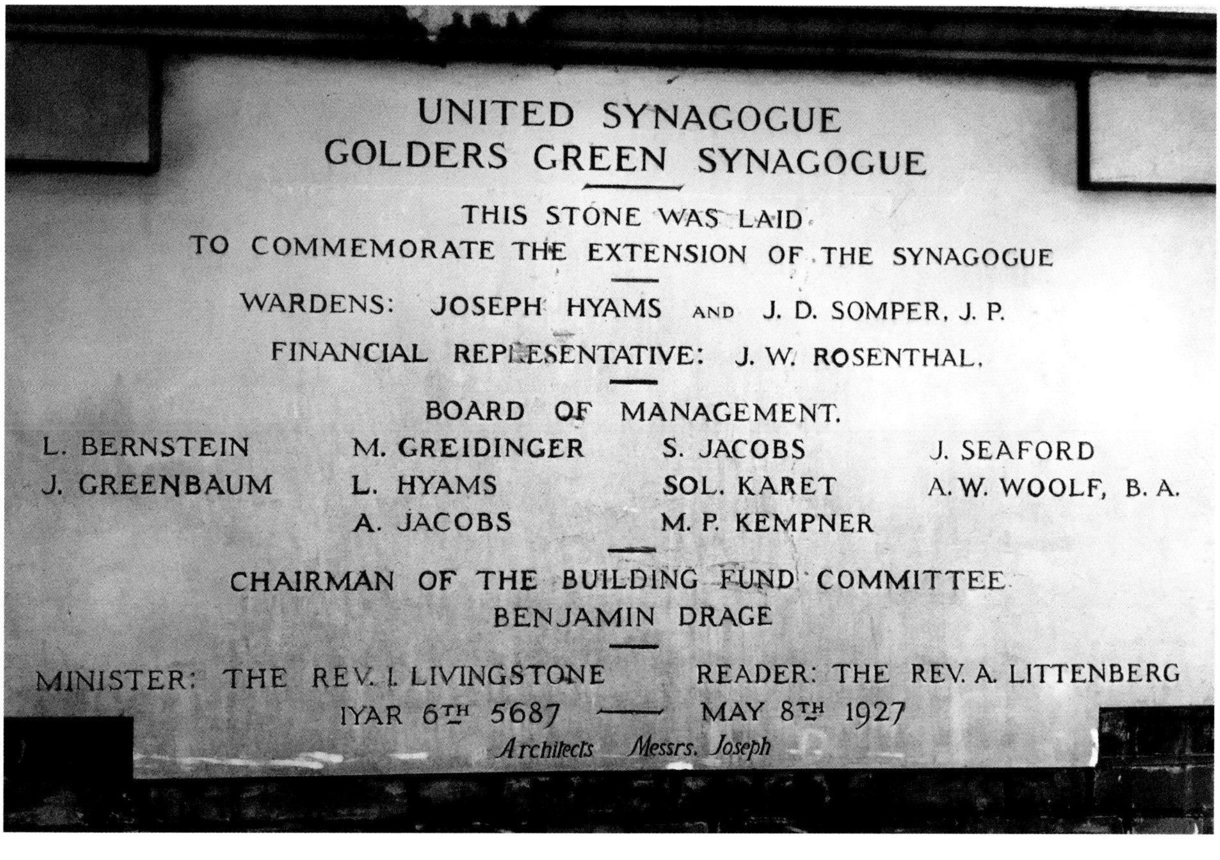

UNITED SYNAGOGUE
GOLDERS GREEN SYNAGOGUE

THIS STONE WAS LAID
TO COMMEMORATE THE EXTENSION OF THE SYNAGOGUE

WARDENS: JOSEPH HYAMS AND J. D. SOMPER, J.P.

FINANCIAL REPRESENTATIVE: J. W. ROSENTHAL.

BOARD OF MANAGEMENT.

L. BERNSTEIN	M. GREIDINGER	S. JACOBS	J. SEAFORD
J. GREENBAUM	L. HYAMS	SOL. KARET	A. W. WOOLF, B.A.
	A. JACOBS	M. P. KEMPNER	

CHAIRMAN OF THE BUILDING FUND COMMITTEE
BENJAMIN DRAGE

MINISTER: THE REV. I. LIVINGSTONE   READER: THE REV. A. LITTENBERG
IYAR 6TH 5687 —— MAY 8TH 1927
Architects Messrs. Joseph

Cohen had been present when the foundation stone had first been laid in October 1921,[87] then again for the first consecration in 1922. A local newspaper reported: 'The service was simple yet most impressive and was followed reverently throughout by the great congregation. The work of the choir, under the direction of Mr Busky was magnificent.'[88] It was attended by members of the wider Jewish community, the United Synagogue, civic dignitaries, and members of other faiths. The Chief Rabbi led the procession of the Torah scrolls three times around the sanctuary, followed by Rev. Livingstone, Rev. A. Littenberg, Dayan Dr Feldman, Dayan Hillman, Dayan Mendelsohn, Sir Robert Waley Cohen, Joseph Hyams, Councillor J. Somper, Councillor J. Rosenthal, Benjamin Drage, Samuel Moses, Joseph Prag JP, Mr. J. Rossdale, Frank Samuel and Lawrence Levy. In his sermon, Chief Rabbi Hertz paid tribute to the Anglican vicar, Rev. Trundle, who had enabled the congregation to use St Alban's Hall.

The new extended building consisted of robing rooms, more storerooms and an area for the choir above the Ark.[89] The pews and paneling were in oak, and the marble steps to the Ark were a gift from Benjamin Drage, a founder and first president of the synagogue. The marble steps, pulpit and Almemar were donated by the Drage family and Mrs Jacobs in memory of Mrs Rose Cohen. Many of the beautiful stained glass windows were installed at this time, donated by various members of the congregation. By now, a total of £54,000 had been spent on building and extending the synagogue since its foundation. During 1927-8, the synagogue's annual income rose from £4,289 per annum to £5,482. The following year, it had risen to £6,036, largely due to an increase in new members. That income came primarily from membership, a significant proportion of which was for seat rental for services. The rental cost of seats varied according to their location within the sanctuary. For example, seat Nos. 123-140 could be rented for £8.8.0. per annum, and seat Nos. 141-255 for £7.7.0 per annum.

The synagogue became a popular place for marriages; sixteen alone were solemnized in the shul in 1928-9. The Entertainment Committee organized numerous social functions to raise funds towards the choir which was a professional paid choir at this time. A number of societies continued the synagogue's support of Jewish revival in Palestine: Keren Hayesod, Jewish National Fund, Women's Zionist Society and the Junior Zionist Society.

The synagogue records show that on the morning of Sunday 11 November 1928, an Armistice Day Service was held in the synagogue. The service began with a reading of Psalm 22, followed by an address, Prayer for the King and Royal Family, Armistice Prayer and a two minute silence. A Memorial Prayer for those fallen in battle was followed by Alenu, the Mourners' Kaddish and concluded with Adon Olam.

In the late 1920s, the issue of competing membership with the Hendon Synagogue, also a constituent of the United Synagogue, came to the fore. In 1928, an agreement was reached between the two shuls, noted in full in the Minute Book:

1 The Hendon Synagogue should not be allowed to take members from the Golders Green side of the Brent (altered afterwards to North Circular Road).
2 To take no defaulting members of the Golders Green Synagogue
3 To take no existing members of the Golders Green Synagogue for a period of five years
4 Officers of the Golders Green Synagogue to be supplied at regular intervals with Hendon's members' names and addresses

At a special meeting of seatholders on 13 January 1929, the congregation appointed its temporary beadle, Mendel Susser, on a permanent basis. His salary was increased to £200 per annum, rising to a maximum of £240. In May that year, the Minute Books note how the congregation presented a silver coffee service to Joseph Hyams in recognition of his past services to the synagogue. In spite of the extension to the synagogue building, overflow services were held in the classrooms for the High Holy Days for non-members who wished to attend. Once again, the building was filled to capacity. The Minutes also mention the arrangements for relatives staying temporarily in the area over the High Holy Days and it was agreed that relatives of members of the congregation, and unmarried sons of members, could be allocated seats in the synagogue.

Once again, the Board of Management's attention was drawn to decorum during the festival services. Jimmy Seaford urged 'something to be done to prevent the incessant conversation during services.'[90] This would remain a constant theme and still continues to trouble the community from time to time today.

As the decade of the 1920s drew to a close, the finances of the synagogue were balanced with a surprising deficit of £286.4s.10d. Benjamin Drage, the synagogue's first president, had stepped down in his role in the community and, in recognition of his service, elected honorary member of the synagogue at a nominal membership of £2.2s. and retained all rights and privileges.

---

[87] The foundation stone itself had been laid in 1921 by Lionel de Rothschild.
[88] *The Hendon, Cricklewood, Golders Green & Mill Hill Times*, 23 October 1927.
[89] This area for the choir was subsequently closed by a false screen and is not visible today.
[90] Minute Book, 4 November 1929.

The 1930s

By 1930, the number of Jews living in north-west London was expanding at a significant rate. Attempts were made to link new smaller congregations to existing established synagogues to enable them to benefit from a qualified minister when they were not yet large enough to engage the services of a minister or Rabbi. The Board of Management expressed the aspiration that 'our synagogue, which is one of the largest and most beautiful of London synagogues, will continue to receive the loyal support of the Jewish inhabitants of the district, and that Golders Green Jewry will continue to go forward in furthering the spiritual welfare of the Jewish community.'[91] Congregations were springing up in Finchley and Highgate as well as Hendon.[92] Jack Greenbaum, chair of the Board of Management at this time, reported that the congregation had loaned Sefrei Torah to the Highgate Synagogue for its consecration service.[93]

In December 1930, the congregation came to a mutual agreement with the new Finchley Hebrew Synagogue. It included a payment of 10/- per annum to Golders Green shul in exchange for Rev. Livingstone preaching occasionally at the Finchley congregation, also conducting marriages, and one of the ministers of Golders Green assisting at funerals and stone-settings. It was agreed that the Finchley congregation could have occasional use of the classrooms at the Golders Green Synagogue for some of its functions.

The decade of the 1930s was marked in Europe by a rapidly changing political landscape that witnessed the rise of Nazism and Adolf Hitler become chancellor of Germany. The impact of Hitler's singling out of Jews to deny them their civil rights was soon felt further afield as Jewish refugees began to arrive in north-west London. Some settled in Golders Green, Swiss Cottage and St. John's Wood. This shift in Jewish population had an impact on the Golders Green Synagogue which, until the 1930s, was unrivalled in the area for membership. New congregations sprung up, as well as purpose-built synagogues erected, which gave Jews a choice of congregation other than the Golders Green Synagogue. In 1934, the Ashkenazi Munk's Synagogue was founded, known as the Golders Green Beth Hamedrash. The influx of refugees altered the nature of Golders Green, which became a much more populated Jewish area, although the densest settlement of German Jewish refugees was around Belsize Park.

Long-term, the birth of new congregations, coupled with the arrival of refugees, would have an impact on the membership of the Golders Green Synagogue, but for now, the congregation enjoyed a large membership. Attendance for High Holy Days and festivals remained high, such that

it necessitated overflow services in the hall. Naomi Rose grew up in the community and remembers the period of the 1930s:

'The Pennine estate used to be Hanley Page aircraft manufacturers. I remember the planes taking off and it being quite frightening because this was new technology. I also remember the aerodrome on Grahame Way. All ladies and girls wore hats to services. I also remember our *cheder* days. I was taught by Mrs Cohen who had been widowed in WW1. Her husband had served in the RAF and been killed in action, and this was how she as a lady without children came to be teaching us. It was clear that the bereavement affected her deeply, but she was a very dedicated teacher. Mrs Cohen was still teaching my children at *cheder* in the 1950s and 60s. Classes for children ran from 10am to 1pm on Sundays, on Tuesdays and Thursdays from 5pm for one hour. Mrs Cohen always started her class at 4.30pm. The headmaster in this period was Mr Busky. During the week, the Jewish children attended Wessex Gardens School. For the children who had not passed the 11+ exam and stayed on at

---

[91] The Annual Report 1931-2.

[92] At a meeting of Board of Management on 19 July 1932: 'The Board of Management confirmed the decision of the Hon. Officers to agree to the proposed new site of the Hendon Synagogue.'

[93] Minute Book, 9 January 1930.

a school locally, Rev. Livingstone led the religious education classes. The synagogue was packed for Kol Nidre, with standing room only. We had to have the children's services in the classrooms and the children didn't go into the shul itself for services.'[94]

Naomi went on to marry Benjamin Rose in the synagogue in 1948. The Rose family were long-standing members and Benjamin Rose had been bar mitzvah in the shul and later became a warden.

In November 1930, Rev. Livingstone, was asked to give a short lecture about the 50,000 Jews who had fought in the Great War, including those from across the British Empire. This was attended by a number of clerics and ministers of different faiths. Catering for the changing needs of the children of the community remained a high priority for Rev. Livingstone. Wessex Gardens Primary School was at that time a very popular choice for the local Jewish children and Rev. Livingstone arranged for the Jewish pupils to go to the synagogue three times a week for their Jewish scripture lessons, as required by the government curriculum. By the late 1930s, the synagogue hall was also periodically used by the Jewish Lads' Brigade.

The number of children attending *cheder* had risen to 154 in 1930, in contrast to 36 in 1917. It now consisted of six classes, five of which were housed in the partitioned hall, and the beginners' class in the Board Room. Classes were taught by Miss Solomon, Mrs Cohen, Mr Busky, Miss Shaer and Mr Orler. Sixteen weddings were solemnized, and eleven bar mitzvahs celebrated in 1930. Curtains for the Ark and a cover for the Reading Desk were given by Mr and Mrs Konskier. Silver bells, a yad and a breastplate were donated by Jeff Bernstein, inscription over the Ark by Mr and Mrs J. Somper, and two stained glass windows by Mr and Mrs Paul in memory of Mr and Mrs Otto.

Women in the Community

Throughout its hundred-year history, the women of the shul have always played a very active part. During the 1930s, the Ladies' Society remained active in its key roles of work within the community, both religious and welfare. Under the auspices of its president Mrs Livingstone, it raised money in 1930 for the Rose Hertz Memorial Fund. It met weekly for its sewing group under the honorary secretary, Mrs G. Cohen of Woodstock Road.

The ladies also took on the role of repairing the synagogue vestments, and making garments for hospitals and the poor. In their wide-ranging charitable work, the women were been able to help the Stepney Jewish Hospital, the Jewish Home of Rest, the Maternity Home and the Stepney After-Care Committee; all this in a period before the establishment of the National Health Service. The

Women's Zionist Society of the synagogue was presided over by Mrs J. Bloch and Miss B. Moshkowitz, and honorary secretary Mrs Livingstone.

It was during the 1930s that a heated debate arose in the congregation over the possible introduction of a mixed choir of men and women for services. According the Halacha (Jewish Law) mixed choirs or women-only choirs are forbidden and it was very unusual for there to be a mixed choir in a United Synagogue associated shul. The idea had been proposed by Sydney Ellis who felt that it would enhance the services and improve attendance. In this, he was supported by Mr I. Lubbock. The Board of Management was not in agreement, with strong opposition presented by Mr Phil Jacobs who maintained that it was against Jewish Law. He said at one particular meeting that: 'its introduction would mean the resignation of some of the oldest members of the synagogue.' Mr M. Landa added to this by saying that he feared it would lead to further reforms and that 'non-Jews admired us only as long as we respected our traditions.' To which response another member of the Board replied that the Chief Rabbi was not against mixed choirs and it was the die-hards such as Phil Jacobs who were driving away many United Synagogue congregants who would then join Reform synagogues.

Rev. Livingstone concurred that a mixed choir could not be prohibited on religious grounds and the current Chief Rabbi had not forbidden it, however he (Rev. Livingstone) took advice from the former Chief Rabbi, Dr

---

Hermann Adler, that 'should it be desired to introduce such a modification into a synagogue, the greatest precaution should be exercised that such introduction do not mar the peace and brotherly union which should exist among the members... It should not take effect unless it has been approved by a decided majority of the members, especially of those who attend the services which will be affected by the proposed alteration.'

The motion was finally withdrawn on grounds that it would offend many regular attendants. The *Jewish Chronicle* ran an article about the debate, with the headline *Mixed Choir Not to Be Introduced: A Heated Discussion.*[95]

The Life of the Community

A snapshot of the issues and life of the congregation are aptly recorded in the congregation's archives, especially the Minute Books. The issue of decorum was raised once again at a meeting presided over by Jack Greenbaum who petitioned synagogue members to 'attend services with their shabbas suits and shabbas hats (Hear, Hear). It looks so bad to see one man called up to the Torah in a soft hat, whilst another wore a silk one.'[96]

Proper conduct, or lack of it, during services was often a matter of concern to the Board of Management. A letter was read from a new member resigning his membership 'on account of the decorum of the synagogue'. To investigate and suggest possible remedies, the congregation decided to do what it did best – appoint a new committee. The sub-committee was therefore appointed, consisting of Hon. Officers of the synagogue, Sol. Josephs, and Messrs. Ellis, H. Hyman, S. Werner and L. Bernstein, to look at how to institute and maintain correct behaviour in services.[97] The sub-committee reported back with a number of recommendations that included:

'Honorary officers and committee representatives to set a good example by refraining from conversation during the service, the appointment of a female

Alderman Sidney Bolsom, JP, warden 1933–7.

beadle, appoint an assistant beadle to prevent conversations during a service, discourage the practice of children leaving the synagogue during the circuit of the Torah scroll(s), encourage the congregation to join in singing with the choir, reading some prayers in English, and not allowing people to enter or leave the synagogue during the opening of the Ark and reading of the Torah... Smoking should not be permitted in the vestibule or within the precincts and grounds of the synagogue.'

These measures must have been successful because no more complaints about decorum were raised for some time.

A young Zionist Society, *Halapid*, was formed and led by Mr S. Harwich and David Meyer, its treasurer Miss F. Landesberger. A New Zionist Society was also established

---

[95] *Jewish Chronicle*, on 26 November 1937.
[96] Quoted from the Annual Report 1931-2, copy in the synagogue archives.
[97] Decided at a meeting held on 31 October 1932.

to promote Zionist ideals in the neighbourhood and to coordinate efforts of societies working for a revival of Jewish life in Palestine. This was presided over by Barnett Janner, Rev. Livingstone, Mr F. Isaacs and Dr Samson Wright.

Between 1930 and 1932, the number of children enrolled in *cheder* had risen to almost 200, necessitating seven classes. Twenty-six boys were bar mitzvah in 1933. Every Wednesday, a Torah study group met in the synagogue classrooms, conducted by Mr Friedlander. The following year, the numbers attending religion classes had risen to 226, with eight classes meeting on a Sunday morning and three on a Wednesday evening. Teachers were Mr B. Busky, Mr M. Harris, Mr S. Somper, Miss J. Manne, Miss S. Solomon, Miss J. Lubin, Mrs M. Cohen and Mrs F. Levene.

A meeting was convened at Golders Green Synagogue between all local synagogues to discuss cooperating in Jewish education classes. This included representatives from the Hendon Synagogue, North-Western Reform Synagogue, Hampstead Garden Suburb Congregation, Golders Green Beth Hamedrash, alongside the director of Jewish Education from the United Synagogue, Herbert Adler. The meeting concluded that it would not be practical to cooperate on religious education of children attending schools in the Borough of Hendon.[98]

Finances had improved for the year 1933-4, such that the annual income for the synagogue amounted to £6,935. 12s. 8d. After all financial commitments had been accounted for, a surplus of £31. 9s. 2d. remained.

Philip Jacobs, warden 1932-3.

With knowledge of the persecution of Jews in Nazi-occupied lands, the Golders Green Synagogue mobilized support for various Zionist causes that aspired to a Jewish homeland in Palestine; the State of Israel not being established until 1948. In 1930, a large meeting of the Jewish Palestine Societies of north-west London was held in the synagogue hall, addressed by Rev. Livingstone. During this period, too, the synagogue acted as the main focal point for the Young Israel Society. The appointment of Hitler as Chancellor of Germany in 1933 provoked a lengthy statement in the Minute Book of the period:

'Profoundly sympathizing with the Jews of Germany on account of the treatment to which they are subjected by reason of their faith and race, the members of the Golders Green Synagogue appeal to the British government to express its horror at the campaign of anti-Jewish oppression and persecution in that country, and to support the demand for freedom and justice to all sections of its inhabitants.'

The congregation wholeheartedly supported the Central British Fund for German Jewry, set up to aid Jewish refugees from Nazi persecution. Mrs Kaplan secured the use of one of the rooms on the synagogue premises for use once a fortnight 'for the making of garments for Jewish refugees from Germany, now in Palestine.' Mr I. Kestenbaum chaired a special appeal committee on behalf of the United Appeal for Polish Jewry. The congregation expressed its disapproval at the United Synagogue stance at the time regarding the Central British Fund for German Jewry and passed the following resolution:

'That this meeting of seatholders of the Golders Green Synagogue deplores the continued failure of the United Synagogue to support the Central British Fund for German Jewry and instructs its representative at Council to move a suitable resolution asking the Hon. officers to donate a substantial sum for the relief of the refugees in the metropolis.'[99]

Barbara Michaels also remembers this period and how members of the congregation helped refugees from Nazi oppression: 'I often went with my mother to collect money from guarantors for the Kindertransport. Members of the Golders Green Synagogue agreed to take refugee children in their homes. One founding member of the shul, Mr Jacobs, took in a refugee from Germany called Herbert Goldsmith [Goldschmidt] who was very active in the life of the shul after the war until his death some seventy years later.'

Later, in the aftermath of Kristallnacht (9/10 November 1938), a Special Emergency meeting of the Board of

---

[98] Meeting held on 16 April 1934.
[99] Passed at the General Meeting on Sunday 19 May 1935.

Top of the Ark and choir area decorated for Shavuot.

Management was convened to discuss the election of three representatives to a committee in north-west London to coordinate local activity on behalf of Jews in Germany.[100]

Congratulations were offered to the congregation's first president, Benjamin Drage, for his Knighthood 'conferred upon him for his public services.' Mr. Drage donated a Bible for use at the pulpit and two bronze book-rests for the lectern. A gift of electric light fittings on the sides of the Ark were donated by Mrs M. Wix and a mantle for a Torah Scroll by Mr A. Kirshenstein. Other donations included a Torah scroll with silver breastplate, pointer and three mantles by the widow and family of Aaron Kirshenstein; lamps for the synagogue and classrooms, donated by Mr H. Kaplan; and a Chuppah given by Mr B. Hartstein for weddings.

Sidney Bolsom and Mr J. Somper were sent congratulations on being elected Aldermen, and Councillor A. Naar for being elected Chairman of the Hendon Urban District Council. A Civic Service was held in his honour in the synagogue. The congregation's contribution to the civic life continued, as in 1933, Alderman Bolsom was appointed Mayor of St. Pancreas. On 7 May 1933, a special service was held in the synagogue, attended by several Mayors of Metropolitan boroughs, Aldermen and councillors.

The synagogue marked important moments in the nation's history. The King's Silver Jubilee was celebrated in the synagogue on Saturday 11 May 1935 by a *Special*

THIS MEMORIAL LAMP
IS LIGHTED TO THE MEMORY OF
ROSE FREEDMAN
(1859-1933)
BY HER SON MYER
WHO DONATED THE
SYNAGOGUE ELECTROLIERS
JANUARY 1938 – SHEVAT 5698
"AN EVERLASTING LIGHT"

---

[100] It was convened on Sunday 4 December 1938.

Service of Prayer and Thanksgiving for George V's Accession to the Throne, which was incorporated into the main Shabbat service, a service attended by a number of local civic dignitaries and clergy of different faiths. The following January, the Minute Book records the sad death of the King and noted: 'a vote of condolence was passed to King Edward on the death of King George, the members standing in silence.'[101]

On 30 July 1935, the Board of Management wrote to Rev. Moise Taschlicky inviting him to become temporary Reader for a maximum of two years on a salary of £450 per annum. Rev. Littenberg had retired as Reader. That same year, the idea of holding a dinner and dance at either the Dorchester in Mayfair or the Savoy Hotel was born. This became an annual fund-raising event known as the Green and Gold Ball. The first such evening was held to raise money for the Reconstruction Fund.

Charitable work continued to be a central part of the community's life. For example, the congregation donated money to the Mayor of Hendon's Cottage Hospital Appeal. On 29 February 1936, Nancie Livingstone, Rev. Livingstone's eldest daughter, organized a Leap Year Ball in aid of the Brady Associated Clubs – the Jewish youth clubs in the East End. It was held at The Brady Girls' Club in Hanbury Street, Whitechapel. The evening included dance, cabaret and an orchestra.

The Joseph Freedman Hall

In 1936, the High Holy Day services for the children were conducted by Mr P. Blackman, and adult overflow services by Mr J. Weinberg of Jews' College. Mr H. Fletcher donated a curtain for the Ark, silver *rimmonim* (bells), a breastplate and pointer in memory of his parents, and the Ladies' Society gave three embroidered mantles for Torah scrolls. Although 1936-7 saw a slight fall in numbers attending the *cheder*, from 200 to 175, the Board of Management felt that the current premises were insufficient to meet the needs of the community. On 27 October 1937, a letter was sent to every member of the shul:

'It has long been felt that the necessity for increased accommodation for literary and social purposes connected with the synagogue was imperative... The number of children on the roll of Religion Classes is approaching 200 again and the matter of classroom accommodation has become a serious problem. Occasions are becoming more frequent when classes have to take their lessons in the synagogue.'

In spite of the extension to the synagogue in 1927, it was still necessary to hold overflow services in the classrooms

Interior of the Joseph Freedman Hall. COURTESY MAURICE SAMUELSON

[101] Minute Book entry 26 January 1936.

The part of the synagogue that was extended in 1927.

and hire St Alban's Hall for the High Holy Days. Building a new hall was offered as a solution, estimated cost between £5,000 and £7,000. The final cost was, of course, much more than original estimates once the project got underway. Plans were submitted to the United Synagogue for consideration, and included not only a communal hall, but new classrooms.[102] The *Jewish Chronicle* reported in May 1938 that progress had been made such that 'it was hoped they would be in use the following year, to be called the Joseph Freedman Memorial Hall. Mr M. Freedman and family had given £15,000 towards the project in memory of his father.'

The project began with the laying the foundation stone on 15 January 1939. Four months later, on 21 May 1939, a special service in the synagogue preceded its opening by Chief Rabbi Dr Joseph Hertz, assisted by Rev. Livingstone and Rev. Taschlicky. The choir was assisted by choirmaster David Levine. Attending too were His Worship the Mayor of Hendon, Councillor H. G. Potter, the Mayoress, and various Aldermen and Councillors. The *Jewish Chronicle* reported that after the service, 'the congregation proceeded to the hall which was declared open for public use by Joseph Freedman, to whom a key was presented by Mr. H. Hyman, the senior warden.' The Mayor spoke about the recent influx of refugees from Nazism and expressed:

'If the service of the synagogue inculcated in these refugees a little of the tradition of the country to which they had come, if it made them feel that they had done with the cruelties from which they had fled and that they were now free, it would be a very good thing.'

The ladies of the congregation were praised for providing excellent food for the reception afterwards.

The Joseph Freedman Hall served a very important role in the life of the community in the coming decades until its demolition in 2012 to make way for the Rimon Jewish Free School. With its theatrical stage and lighting, the hall became also a popular venue for *bar mitzvah* and wedding receptions.

It was also used by a wide range of organisations, including the Jewish Friendship Club, where people over the age of 60 met on a Wednesday under the aegis of the indefatigable Anita Daniels. It was the scene of quiz nights, Purim celebrations, Zionist meetings, prize-givings and overflow services.

The Dunstan Road synagogue enjoyed nearly two decades without serious competition in the Golders Green area. It accommodated people with a wide range of religious observance. But all that was about to change during and after the Second World War when more observant orthodox refugees arrived from the continent. They did not relate to the, then, religious ethos of the Golders Green Synagogue and started their own communities.

---

[102] Minute Book entry, 7 March 1938.

CHAPTER 6

The Second World War

TWENTY YEARS AFTER the Great War, Europe was plunged into another world war. The Golders Green Synagogue remained deeply concerned about the fate of its co-religionists in Nazi-occupied countries. The community that had already actively helped refugee causes in the 1930s, continued its support of the British Fund for World Jewry. It also held services of intercession in the synagogue for victims of Nazism, and hosted numerous Zionist groups and meetings on the premises. Members of Golders Green Synagogue enlisted in the Armed Forces and made their own contribution to the defeat of Nazism. Those who died in action are commemorated on the synagogue's War

Memorial fountain in the vestibule. Amongst them were Milton Bender, Joseph Bender, Leslie Israel and Peter Robinson. The community's own minister, Rev. Livingstone served as chairman of the District Committee for Defence for Golders Green for the duration of the war.

The impact of the Second World War was felt by the community in a number of ways. Numerous unexploded bombs and incendiary devices fell on Golders Green from the Luftwaffe bombing raids, vividly shown by a special map which exists in the Hendon Archives. 'Outside Eagle Lodge in the Golders Green Road and Russell Gardens were hit,' recalls Naomi Rose. 'Many people were evacuated to the countryside during the blitz. My family was evacuated not far, to an aunt in Finchley.' Rev. Livingstone's daughter, Barbara Michaels, also recalls:

> 'During the war, we had an Anderson shelter in our garden at 15 Golders Gardens. Then in 1941, a time-delayed bomb landed in the street, but did not go off. Houses in our street were evacuated, including ours. Just two days later, a landmine was dropped on the same spot and exploded. Nine houses in our street were destroyed. It was a lucky escape. Everyone survived because they had been evacuated from the previous bomb. We lost all our possessions, including family photographs, and were only able to retrieve a few items from the rubble. We were offered temporary accommodation with friends in Welwyn Garden City where, in the end, we stayed for two and a half years. My father stayed behind in Golders Green for his congregation and lodged with a member of the community in

Wedding of Denise and Norman Williams, 21 November 1943.

United Synagogue—ק"ק כנסת ישראל

ADMISSION CARD
GOLDERS GREEN SYNAGOGUE,
DUNSTAN ROAD, N.W.11.

HIGH HOLYDAY SERVICES
5705—1944

NEW YEAR. ראש השנה
Eve of Rosh Hashanah, Sunday, 17th September .... 6.30 p.m.
1st day Rosh Hashanah, Monday, 18th September .... 8.0 a.m.
Evening Service, Monday, 18th September .... 6.30 p.m.
2nd day Rosh Hashanah, Tuesday, 19th September .... 8.0 a.m.

DAY OF ATONEMENT. יום כפור
Fast commences 6.25 p.m.
Kol Nidre, Tuesday, 26th September .... 6.35 p.m.
Yom Kippur, Wednesday, 27th September .... 8.0 a.m.
Concluding Service—Neilah .... 6.0 p.m.
Fast terminates 7.28 p.m.

GENTLEMAN'S SEAT No. 196 P.T.O.

COURTESY: DR SIMON COHEN

Exterior of the synagogue.

Riverside Drive. My sister worked for Rothschild's bank. Then we were fortunate in that the council requisitioned a flat for us in Golders Green, first in Gloucester Court and then Eagle Lodge. At the school where I taught, I remember having to take the children down into the Anderson shelter after the sirens went off. It was a very difficult time.'

In 1948, Barbara married Dick Michaels in a ceremony conducted by her father. Rationing was still in force and she, like so many other couples, had no white wedding dress but bought a practical outfit that she could wear again. Her sister Nancie married Seymour Craig, a practicing barrister, in the synagogue on 29 July 1942, officiated by her father Rev. Livingstone.[103] They settled in Golders Green and Seymour Craig later became a warden of the shul, and he and Nancie remained working tirelessly for the community until their deaths.

There was another consequence of the bombing of London, as recalled by Barbara Michaels: 'The large East End Jewish community was also affected by the heavy blitz. Many were bombed-out of the East End and came to Golders Green to resettle temporarily. They were young and married with children. They kept their membership of the East End shuls, but attended our services and that affected our income.'

Because of blackout regulations, during the winter, the *Ma'riv* or evening services were held in the afternoon rather than the evening. Discussions continued periodically throughout the war about use of the synagogue, hall and classrooms after blackout hours.[104] 'Because of the Blackout Regulations, it was not possible to completely darken the synagogue windows and the Kol Nidre service was held in the afternoon,' says Naomi Rose, who lived through this period. 'In the first year of the war, the High Holy Days were extraordinary because, not only did the congregation have overflow services in the hall, but arrangements were made for extra services in the classrooms for the German-speaking refugees.' The Choir Committee proposed interviewing refugee-chorister Mr. Raguchanski for a temporary position, at an honorarium of £1 a month.

The United Synagogue issued guidelines to congregations in the event of an air raid siren being sounded during High Holy Day Services. Golders Green Synagogue had a rota of fire-watch duties for the building in case it was hit. Fortunately, the synagogue suffered no damage during the blitz. In 1941, the United Synagogue sent a letter to the synagogue outlining the fact that the community had made no provision to safeguard in any special way the memorial windows of the synagogue and that this should be carried out.

The influx of refugees had begun to change the nature

---

[103] At the time of the marriage, Seymour Craig (the son of Immanuel Jacob Cohen) was serving in the RAF – it being the middle of the war.
[104] Blackout Regulations began to affect the Wednesday evening Hebrew classes such that a discussion took place on moving the time of the class.

OUR NEW BRANCH

Will be Opened on MONDAY, JANUARY 23rd

FOR THE SALE OF THE

Choicest High-Class Kosher Meat & Poultry

— *A Special Department will also be opened for the sale of* —
KOSHER PROVISIONS AND DELICATESSEN

Advert for kosher butcher.

of the Golders Green area. The synagogue received a request from the Refugee Club in April 1940 to hold its own Seder on first night of Passover in the Joseph Freedman Hall. The Minute Book notes the discussion by the Board of Management: 'A lengthy and considerable discussion ensued, however, as to the procedure that ought to be adopted by the participants in the Seder, strong divergence of opinions were expressed. It was decided that the secretary convey to the sponsors that it was the hope of the Board that English might be used by the person directing the Seder, without however, in any way suggesting this as a condition for the granted use of the hall.'[105]

Permission was granted for the club to use the premises, conditional on one member of the Board being given a seat on its committee.[106] The congregation received a Torah scroll for safekeeping from Germany from Miss Kate Stern. In giving the scroll back to her in 1964, Miss Stern subsequently donated it to the Middlesex New Synagogue at 39 Bessborough Road in Harrow.

The Minute Book reflects, too, the concerns and conditions of a community living through the war. For example, there was mounting anxiety over the lack of attendance for services, largely explained by wartime conditions and evacuations. The synagogue responded how it knew best – by forming a new committee called the Publicity Committee. Its inaugural meeting took place on 25 June 1940. Present were Messrs. H. Hyman, A. Taylor, S. Ellis, I. H. Levy, John Golding, Miss C. Balaban and Rev. Livingstone and Rev. Taschlicky, with apologies received from Messrs S. Josephs, S. London, Jacob Greenbaum, S.S.

Levin, A Rabson, L. Elton, Mrs Livingstone and Miss Livingstone. The purpose of the committee was outlined:

'To make contact with the members of the congregation and bring home to them sense of obligation and responsibility to the Synagogue' and 'awaken religious and communal sense which was becoming dormant owing to war conditions.'

The next meeting of the committee was scheduled for Sunday 21 July 1940, at which its members discussed the 'absence of Jewish life and environment now facing many children owing to evacuation, coupled with the defection of many members, made the outlook for the future very serious.' The financial status of the community was also becoming a cause for concern. Revenue had fallen by £500 per annum from membership fees, owing to at least 150 members having been evacuated out of the area.

In 1940, founding member Sol Karet completed fifty years of unbroken membership of the United Synagogue, twenty-five years of which he had given in service to the Golders Green congregation as a continuous member of the Board. On the news of his death in 1941, a special emergency meeting of the Board of Management was convened to express its feelings at his passing. The meeting recorded that: 'It places on record its profound appreciation of the devoted and zealous services rendered by Mr. Karet to the synagogues over a period of 25 years. The Board mourns the loss of an esteemed colleague, and his memory will long live with them as a sincere and indefatigable collaboration.'[107]

---

[105] Minute Book entry, 14 April 1940.
[106] Minute Book entry, 3 June 1940.
[107] Meeting held on Sunday 26 January 1941.

Arthur Taylor, warden 1943-7.

Wartime Community Life

Reconstructing the life of the congregation during this period is possible because of surviving Minute Books and correspondence in the synagogue archives. It reveals the challenges of war for a congregation that sought to remain as active as possible. One impact was that there was no need for overflow services during High Holy Days for the first time since anyone could remember. All worshippers could be accommodated in the main synagogue. The warden reported:

'The general functions of the synagogue are being carried on in as far a normal manner as is possible under present circumstances. Our Sabbath Services are quite well attended, although not by many of our members. Weekday evening services have now been discontinued, as it is impossible to obtain a Minyan at an hour at which it is possible to have the service. They will re-commence as soon as the days begin to lengthen again.'[108]

Approval was given for one of the upper classrooms to be used as a local ARP Rest Room. A Junior Cadet Corps had been formed and met regularly in the hall.

From the outbreak of war on 3 September 1939 until

the end of hostilities on 8 May 1945, there were no fewer than 367 wartime weddings in the synagogue, all officiated by Rev. Livingstone who celebrated 25 years as the community's minister in 1941.

The women continued their charitable work and met on a regular basis; much of their activities relating to the war effort. Within the wider congregation, a staggering £1,665 was raised for the Board of Deputies Appeal. The congregation donated £5 to the Communal *Mikveh* Committee. The choir continued to be led by David Levine, with an agreement that the choir boys be paid 2/6 every month. Mr. Levine received an annual salary of £30 a year as professional choirmaster. The Tenor received 10/- per month and the Bass £1 per month. Additional payments were made for High Holy Day Services. Mr. Large donated the generous sum of £10 to the choir fund. 'Mr Bailey raised the question of the indecorous and noisy behaviour of certain members during the Shabbat morning services.'[109] Nothing seemed to have changed from previous complaints. Mr Taylor reported to one meeting on the loss by theft of the Chanukah Menorah, and the curtain in the hall by fire. In June 1942, the first of the special Children's Shabbat Services were held, conducted by Mr. Goldstein.

An entry in the Minute Book for 5 July 1942 notes: 'The Secretary had been called to HM Forces. The Honorary officers had consulted at an early date in order that the administration work of the Synagogue should not be interrupted that Mrs E. Harris be appointed secretary.' Between them, members of the Board collected £15.15s. 0d. for Nancie Livingstone on her wedding. Mrs A. Paul donated a Sifrei Torah to the congregation, and news was circulated that Mr Barclay had been elected to the Council of the Stepney Borough.

During 1943, the Joseph Freeman Hall was made available for the distribution of new ration books. The High Holy Day Services had once again overflow services which were well attended on account of the number of personnel from the Armed Forces. In particular, Golders Green families welcomed American Jewish soldiers who were in need of hospitality for Shabbat or festivals. One particular success story was that of a young soldier called Sammy Shechter from the Lower East Side of New York. Sammy and his friends were offered hospitality by Daisy and Alfred Woolf. Alfred served as chairman of almost every committee of the shul at some point, and was not only its president, but also in the 1970s as President of the United Synagogue. He also ran the Jewish Cadet Corps for boys before they were old enough to be conscripted. The Woolfs' house in Ambrose Avenue was always open to streams of visitors who passed through, including American soldiers. Sammy became a great favourite in the Woolf household and when he met his future wife, Marie Isaacs, he turned to Daisy for guidance. Marie was the only child of parents who were both deaf and dumb, although

---

[108] Report, 9 November 1941.
[109] Minute Book entry, 25 January 1942.

Outing of synagogue classes to Bachad farm Thaxted, 5 Sept 1943. COURTESY: JEREMY MANUEL

Association of Jewish Youth Cup Final, 1945.

she herself had no hearing or speaking impairment. Daisy and Alfred helped arrange the wedding in loco parentis for both bride and groom. The Shechters revisited Golders Green Synagogue many times after their return to the USA, and many of the prayerbooks used in the 1960s and 70s were donated by Sammy in honour of Daisy and Alfred Woolf.

During wartime, the special Children's Services in the classrooms were very successful, and Mr. A. Hyams appointed new headmaster for classes. Mr S. Josephs offered the gift of a tablet to be inscribed with the names of members and sons of members now serving on HM Forces. In honour of the Chief Rabbi's 70th birthday, the congregation donated £3. 3s. to the Hertz Forest, and £1.1s. to the Jewish Institute for the Blind in Jerusalem.[110]

By 1943, in spite of the number of children who had been evacuated out of London due to the blitz, the religion classes still boasted over a hundred children, with around 70 of them attending Wessex Gardens Primary School. Kosher lunches were served for the children of the school in the synagogue hall, who were brought to it by coaches. One child asked his mother one day: 'Do they call us koshers because we go for our dinner in coaches?'

Tony Lytton, grandson of the one-time Chazan Rev. Littenberg, recalls his bar mitzvah at Golders Green Synagogue in 1943 in which 'the service was attended by lots of servicemen.'

Golders Green Jewish Youth Club

One of the most memorable aspects of the wartime life of the shul was the formation of the hugely successful youth club for the area, not just for synagogue members. The Golders Green Jewish Youth Group began its life in May 1943 with a membership of 150, led by David Manuel (a wholesale fruitier and vegetable trader in Covent Garden),[111] Mr A. Taylor, Alfred Woolf and Mark Goldwater who acted as honorary secretary. Within two months, membership had increased to 350 boys and girls. The club was open five nights a week for ages 10 to 18 year olds. Activities included boxing, swimming, photography, dancing, debating, dramatics, keep-fit, and cricket.

The club's official opening took place in the Joseph Freedman Hall at 5.30 p.m on Sunday 18 July 1943.[112] Ten minutes prior to the opening service, there was an inspection and Guard of Honour for the Mayor of Hendon, Alderman J. Copestake, JP, provided by the 2nd Cadet Battalion Royal Fusiliers, under the command of Lt. Alfred Woolf, and the Hampstead Garden Suburb Company under the command of Jnr Commandant B. Livingstone. Standing in the porch to greet the Mayor and Mayoress were Mr David Manuel, Mark Goldwater, Mr A. Hecker, Joseph Freedman, Philip Taylor, Dr & Mrs I. Feldman, Mr

Michael Manuel.

The Chairman and Committee . . . of the Golders Green Jewish Youth Club request the pleasure of your Company at the Inaugural Opening of the Club to be held at Joseph Freedman Hall, Dunstan Road, N.W.11. on Sunday, July 18th. 1943 at 5 p.m. prompt.

His Worship the Mayor of Hendon has kindly consented to attend.

: PLEASE BRING THIS CARD WITH YOU :

& Mrs Hyman Jacobs, Rev & Mrs Isaac Livingstone, Rev. Taschlicky, Mr & Mrs Arthur Taylor, and Mr & Mrs Alfred Woolf. Other civic members who attended were Alderman and Mrs A. Naar, Councillor and Mrs Perkins, Alderman and Miss Richardson, Councillor and Mrs Hirshfield and Mr. Ramsey. The first president of the club, Joseph Freedman, declared it open and handed over a cheque for 50 guineas for the purchase of equipment. Rev. Livingstone offered a Prayer of Consecration, followed by speeches from a number of dignitaries, including the Mayor of Hendon. The ceremony concluded with the National Anthem.

This was the middle of the war; a reminder of which can be found amongst the papers of the club. There is a leaflet which offers guidance during an air raid:

---

[110] Minute Book entry, 10 January 1943.

[111] David Manuel married Adelaide Comer, daughter of Saul Comer.

[112] I am grateful to Jeremy Manuel for kindly lending me the papers and photographic archive about the Jewish Youth Club.

'In the event of alerts or air raids, it is the management's desire to act in accordance with your wishes. For your information there are Air-raid shelters attached to the rear of the Club premises which are electrically heated, and in the event of an alert or raid, it is our intention to marshal all those members present in the club to these shelters.'

The Mayor and Mayoress of Hendon open the Golders Green Jewish Youth Club, Sunday 18 July 1943, escorted by rev. Livingstone. Courtesy: Jeremy Manuel.

The club was incredibly active and organised a variety of activities, including a Broadcasting Group which met regularly to discuss topical issues. Amongst the subjects debated were: whether the House of Lords should be abolished, do newspapers influence public opinion, and whether there should be equal pay for equal work. The latter caused 'one of the most heated debates for some time,' wrote Max Brenner in his summary of the activities at the time.[113] That particular debate centred primarily around family life, and in particular that equal pay was essential in cases where a woman's husband was serving in the armed forces. Numerous plays and dramatic performances were staged with music. Amongst those who took part in the performances were Michael Manuel, Lucille Lewis, Barbara Williamson, Harry Green, Leon Harris, Jack Marks, Leila Landau and Shirley De Groot.

On the evening of 18 December 1943, the club staged a performance of Oscar Wilde's *The Importance of Being Ernest* in the Joseph Freedman Hall, produced by Miss Rahna Horne and proceeds collected for the Red Cross. It was the first serious production that the club undertook, with scenery designed by Donald Marks, and the lead role of Ernest played by Dennis Toff. Later performances included George Bernard Shaw's *Pygmalion,* produced under the direction of Miss Rahna Horne and performed on 6 & 7 January 1945. Also, *Berkeley Square* in aid of the Golders Green Jewish Youth Club Building Fund.[114] Sponsorship for the accompanying brochure was given by various businesses, including Chas. Barclay Ltd, Manuels of Covent Garden, T. Presky & Son of Lexington Square, and Castle Cleaners Ltd of Circus Road, St John's Wood.

Amongst the club's charitable work was the adoption of a children's hostel called *La Chaurniere de Savoie* in France which housed children suffering from various kinds of lung conditions. Under the initiative of Shirley de Groot, Myrna Condon, Jeanette Davidson and Michael Woolf, parcels of clothing were collected for the hostel. In November 1943, they were able to dispatch twelve bulky parcels to the children. Underpinning this work was the belief that they were 'tied together by the common bond of Jewry.' It was reported:

'At the close of the meeting, 75% of those present made a violent dash to the desk where Joan Goldwater was holding a list of names of children to be adopted. There were 33 names on that certain list and within half an hour, 33 children had gained pen friends and guardians.' Letters were sent to the adopted children because they not only need 'clothes, food and other necessities, but they need a little human sympathy and understanding.'[115]

---

[113] Copy survives in papers lent to the author by Jeremy Manuel.
[114] Performed on 12 & 13 January 1946.
[115] Report amongst the papers relating to the club.

Golders Green Jewish Youth Club's performance of Pygmalion:
Top row, l to r: Mona Caller, Leon Harris, Betty Horne;
Middle row, l to r: Louis Marks, Shirley De Groot, Ronald Ross;
Last row, l to r: Basil Cohen, Joyce Levene, Murray Goldstein.

Theatrical performances by the Golders Green Jewish Youth Club. COURTESY: JEREMY MANUEL

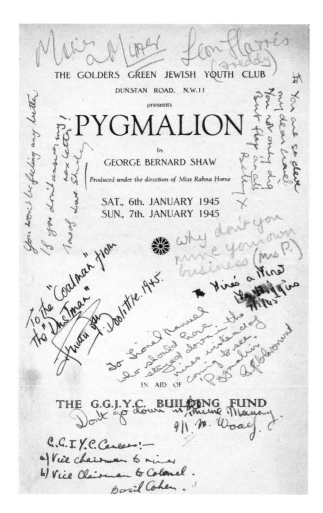

The various groups within the club were headed by: George Dessar (Boxing & Keep-fit), Miss Rahna Horne (Dramatics), Leonard Golding (Discussion and Debating Group), Miss Bobby Jay (Arts and Craft), Jack Dessar (swimming), Canteen (Harry Woolf), Edward Goldston (Outdoor Sports), Herman Spiers and Rev. Taschlicky (Choir) and Eddie Flinter (Finance). The closing comment in the AGM Minutes is interesting and demonstrates the youth's support of the war effort: 'the Chairman reminded those present that the Forces' Comforts' Fund was getting low and was being wholly supported by members themselves.' A list followed of members of the Golders Green Jewish Youth Group who were serving in the Armed Forces: Aubrey Aaronson (Merchant Navy), Monty Gersch (army), Alan Curschenburg (army), Cyril Waterman (RAF), Norman Fox (RAF), Cyril Gersch (RAF) and Ivor Susser (army). The meeting wished them 'good luck and God's speed.'

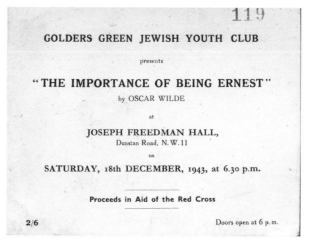

Victory in Europe

The first AGM of the youth club was held on 18 June 1944, chaired by David Manuel. Acknowledgement was given to the fact that Sir Robert Waley Cohen had agreed to accept the presidency of the club. A summary of the year's events was given and mention of the donation of many gifts throughout the year, including a silver cup from Jack Dessar. The surviving Minute Book for the club records its aims and objectives: 'To afford opportunities for the youth of Golders Green district to meet their fellow members of the community, and to spend useful leisure hours in various sections of the club after school or work.'

David Manuel's resume was followed by a speech from Mark Goldwater who confirmed that the membership still remained at around 300 boys and girls, excluding what he termed 'the Juvenile section'. He reported that the average Sunday evening event was attended by 60 to 80 youngsters, although it frequently reached 200. Mention was made of air raids:

> 'Air raid precautions were taken, and at the first air raid warning, members were marshalled by the managers and taken straight into the shelters and remained there until the All-clear was sounded.'[116]

In February 1944, the Rev. W. W. Simpson addressed the Board of Management on the subject of Jewish and Christian relations. Rev. Simpson was a founding member of the Council of Christians and Jews which had been established in 1942 to improve the relationship between Jews and Christians, particularly at a time when the scale of the Holocaust was beginning to be known. Rev. Simpson outlined the aims, objects and purpose for joint activity, to create an atmosphere in which anti-Semitism cannot exist.

When the Allies landed on the beaches of Normandy on D-Day, 6 June 1944, there was new hope that the Nazi regime was on the verge of defeat. Yet it would be almost another year before that was a complete reality.

One of the most touching entries in the congregation's Minute Book is an appeal from the Chief Rabbi, Rev. Dr. J. Hertz, to synagogues to 'donate one or more Torah Scrolls in the reconstruction of Jewish communal life in liberated territories on the Continent.' The Golders Green

---

[116] Quoted from the club's Minute Book, now in the keeping of Jeremy Manuel.

Synagogue approached owners who had lent the congregation Torah scrolls to enquire whether they would offer the scrolls to communities in Europe. That same year, 1994, Alfred Woolf suggested the introduction of bat mitzvah for girls that would be preceded by a two-year course in Hebrew and religion. This was an almost unprecedented innovation within the Jewish orthodox community since the idea that a ceremony for girls, which somehow had links to a bar mitzvah, was generally frowned upon in mainstream shuls of the United Synagogue.[117] In May, Hendon Borough Council was approached with a view to replacing the iron railings at the rear of the synagogue which separate the premises from the public park behind it.

On 8 May 1945, VE Day was celebrated. Congregant Edna Martin remembers that her father, Abraham Sievers, became *Chatan Torah* for Simchat Torah in 1945, and also recalls celebrating the end of the war by 'having a great party and making all the cakes, biscuits and sweetmeats at home. This meant cadging many ingredients from friends because there was still rationing.'

Six years of war was over, and the Nazi regime that had annihilated six million Jews and five million others had been completely defeated. The following day, Wednesday 9 May 1945, the Golders Green Jewish Youth Club held a Service of Thanksgiving for the victory in Europe. During the service, a number of psalms were recited, and a Memorial Prayer was read in Hebrew by Basil Cohen and in English by Lionel Manuel.

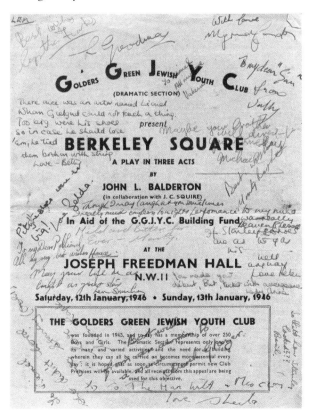

The relief at the end of six years of hostilities was tangible. A whole nation celebrated on the streets of London and in towns and villages. But for many, this was tempered by the knowledge of the casualties of war. Those from the Golders Green Synagogue who lost their lives in action are commemorated on the special War Memorial in the vestibule. From the Second World War, the following men are remembered:

Pilot Officer Milton Harold Bender
Flight Sergeant Joseph Bender, died 17 June 1944
Aubrey L. Bernstein, died 7 July 1945
Flight Sergeant Basil S. Felsenstein, died 15 January 1945
Sergeant Gerald C. Felsenstein, died 12 March 1943
Officer Kenneth Geller, died February 1943
Lt. Herbert Haltrecht, died 23 March 1945
Pilot Officer Aubrey A. Horne, died 27 August 1941
Flying Officer Leslie Israel, died 13 November 1943
2nd Lt. Alroy H. Karamelli, died 22 November 1941
Capt. Simmon Latutin, died 31 December 1944
2nd Lt. Daniel Lawrence, died December 1942
Jack C. Maissel, died September 1943
Warrant Officer John D. Pincus, 19 July 1944
Flying Officer Peter S. M. Robinson, died 19 August 1944
Gnr. Norman Wallach, died 28 February 1945

---

[117] The Minutes do not record the date when Bat Mitzvah was introduced into the Golders Green community, although in 1950, Alfred Woolf would again raise the issue of extending education for girls around the time of their Bat Mitzvah.

MATZO RAMBLE   APRIL 2nd 1945

Above: Thanksgiving Service for Victory in Europe for Golders Green Jewish Youth Club.

Right: Shirley De Groot.

Information is available on only some of the above. Pilot Officer Milton Harold Bender of 460 RAF Squadron was the son of Samuel and Rose Bender, awarded the DFC, died 10 April 1944, aged 20, and is buried in Esbjerg (Fourfelt) Cemetery. Twin brothers F/Sgt Basil S. Felsenstein and Sgt Gerald Cecil Felsenstein both died in action, the sons of Arthur and Ada Felsenstein. Basil was serving with the Royal Air Force Volunteer Service 82 Squadron, and is buried in Gauhati War Cemetery. Flying Officer Leslie Israel of the Royal Air Force Volunteer Service 192 Squadron, who died on 13 November 1943, the son of Isadore and Cissie Israel of Cricklewood, is buried in Willesden Jewish Cemetery, London. Warrant Officer John David Pincus, the son of Capt. Paul Pincas (of the Army Dental Corps) and Myrtle Pincus of Cricklewood, died in action on 19 July 1944, aged 22. He was serving with the Royal Air Force Volunteer Service 602 Squadron, and is buried in Ranville War Cemetery in Normandy.

THE WINNER of "TALENT COMPETITION" 1944

SHIRLEY DE GROOT.

Ramble, 1945.

The Immediate Post-War Period

For Anglo-Jewry, the beginning of January 1946 saw the passing of Chief Rabbi Dr Hertz, one of the most influential Chief Rabbis and a man respected and revered throughout the whole of Anglo-Jewry and within the wider community. Golders Green Synagogue sent the following to the Chief Rabbinate office that the congregation:

'Unites with all other synagogues in recording their great bereavement by the passing of the Very Rev. Dr. J. Hertz. The members of the Golders Green Synagogue – which he consecrated 24 years ago, and which he visited on a number of occasions – will reverence his memory throughout their days and will never forget the service which he rendered to Anglo-Jewry and to the larger community of Israel. The influence of his life work will go on and be an inspiration to many generations in Israel... The deep sympathy of Golders Green Jewry is extended to the members of Dr Hertz's family and indeed to Jewry as a whole.'[118]

In April 1946, the congregation presented an inscribed silver cigarette box to Myer Harris for serving as secretary for 10 years. Overflow services were needed again for the High Holy Day; one for adults and one for children's services. The war may have ended the previous year, but many men and women had yet to be demobbed. The

Minute Book notes for the High Holy Days: 'Three rows of seats to be reserved in the synagogue for Service and Ex-service men.'

Immediately after the war, the community was once again supporting another fight – the fight to establish the State of Israel, which was finally realized in 1948. Golders Green Synagogue held its own events in support of the Zionist cause. The Joseph Freedman Hall became the scene of huge fundraising bazaars, organized by a committee that consisted of members from Alyth Gardens Reform Synagogue and the more strictly orthodox London Beth Hamidrash. These bazaars were so successful that the Golders Green Synagogue eventually formed its own highly successful charity events that raised huge sums of money for good causes.

In 1948, the State of Israel was born amidst much rejoicing at Golders Green. However, feelings of excitement and elation were not universal. Edna Martin recalls: 'Emotions ran high when the State of Israel was born but at the end of a Shabbat morning service, when a spontaneous outbreak of Hatikvah came, some members of the Board walked out. Two brothers, Professor Samson Wright and Aaron Wright, who were members of the shul and very staunch supporters of the State, were met on the way home. They were in tears of joy at the news of the birth of the State of Israel.'

A Habonim group was started immediately post-war; its *madrich* (leader) Raphael Neuberg. 'It thrived,' says Edna Martin, 'as local Jewish youngsters enjoyed its activities

[118] Dated 21 January 1946.

Golders Green Jewish Youth Club Ramble, 4 June 1944.

including summer camps in the countryside and support of Israel which meant we were able to learn a lot of Hebrew. Several members of that group eventually made aliyah to Israel.'

The semi-Jubilee of the Synagogue was celebrated on 12 October 1947 with a Service of Thanksgiving, conducted by Rev. Livingstone, and Rev. Taschlicky. Prominent among the non-Jewish guests were the Mayor of Hendon, Alderman W. R. Clements, the Town Clerk, Mr. L. Worden, and several local Councillors and Rotary members.

During the service, the Ark was opened by the Hon. Ewen S. Montague and the Senior Warden, Alfred Woolf. Three circuits of the synagogue were made with the Sifrei Torah, which were carried by Rev. Taschlicky, Dayan M. Lazarus, Rev. Livingstone, the Hon. Ewen Montague, Messrs. Alfred Woolf and Charles Barclay (Wardens), Mr M. Horne (Financial Representative), Sir Benjamin Drage, and Messrs. J. Seaford, J. Greenbaum, R. Jacobs, S. Josephs, S. London, H. Hyman, A. Tayler and A. Silverman. During the service, a special prayer was read by the Deputy for the Chief Rabbi, Dayan M. Lazarus, which was 'very much appreciated by a large congregation of members and guests.'

After the service, a reception was held in the Joseph Freedman Hall and the classrooms. Alfred Woolf introduced the speakers, amongst whom were the Mayor of Hendon, Alderman W.R. Clemens, the Hon. Ewen S.

Montague, Rev. Livingstone, Charles Barclay and Sir Benjamin Drage. As mementos for the occasion, presentations were made to Rev. Livingstone, Rev. Taschlicky and Mendel Susser. It was noted: 'In spite of the great difficulties experienced in catering for such large numbers in these days of austerity, a memorable afternoon was spent in recording another milestone in the history of our Synagogue.'[119]

At the AGM of the synagogue on 9 May 1948, the new chairman, Alfred Woolf made an appeal for donations for the Joint Palestine Appeal. To meet the needs of the large youth section of the congregation, Rev. M. Myerovitch was appointed youth minister to 'devote himself entirely to the cultural and religious needs of the young people.' His work was appreciated such that it was later noted that the 'character of the club was developing successfully into that of a Jewish Club.' The classes outing had proved such a success that this was to become an annual event for the young people.

The status of the ladies of the congregation is raised now and again at Board of Management meetings. At one such meeting on 16 Sept 1948, a discussion took place about 'the enfranchisement of lady members'. A Resolution was put forward: 'That this meeting has no objection to the enfranchisement of lady members.' The motion was defeated on a show of hands. It was to be a decade before

---

[119] Reported in the Minutes of meeting on 30 November 1947.

women got the vote and several decades before they held positions on the Board.

At a meeting held on 18 November 1948, a vote of congratulations was offered to Rev. Taschlicky 'upon his forthcoming marriage.' Other factors mentioned in the life of the synagogue in the post-war period includes a list of donations: a set of silver and a Reading Desk cover from Mrs Werner in memory of her husband, and a Silver Salver from Mrs Bolsom in memory of her husband.

During 1949, the synagogue raised £1500 for the Joint Palestine Appeal, provoking a comment from the chairman that 'this figure is not entirely satisfactory.'

As the community was about to enter another decade, the age-old issue of conduct during services was raised again. The Minutes noted: 'The question of decorum during the High Holy Days was raised, and it was agreed that the Secretary should arrange for Commissionaires to be on duty in front of the synagogue and in the courtyard.' It was a problem that simply was not going away and would be raised again in the coming years.

The synagogue Memorial to Six Million Jewish Victims of the Holocaust.

CHAPTER 7
The 1950s and 1960s

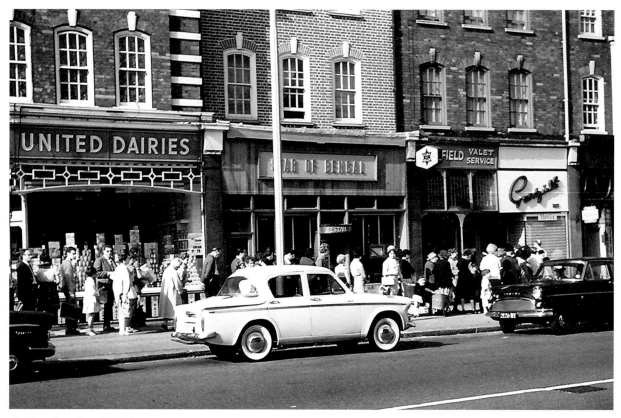

Golders Green Road, 1950s. COURTESY: HENDON LIBRARY & ARCHIVE

BY THE 1950s, the membership of the synagogue comprised mainly businessmen in various trades: furriers, jewellers, tailors, milliners and box manufacturers; and a small number of professionals. Golders Green Road was still a popular, smart shopping area, vibrant and with a number of clothes stores. The synagogue enjoyed a period of growth, with over 200 children in the Hebrew and religion classes. Services were still 'high church' and conducted by officials in canonicals. Formal top hats were worn by the wardens. It was one of the few synagogues that still had a full time Beadle whose responsibilities included decorum at services and calling up for the reading from the Torah.[120] This era saw the retirement of Rev. Livingstone and the arrival of Rabbi Dr Eugene Newman, and the Lebetkin Hall replace the old wooden succah in the grounds behind the shul.

867 Finchley Road. COURTESY OF JONATHAN GRODZINSKI

[120] The Beadle was Mendel Susser, who owned a local kosher wine shop.

During the first year of a new decade, communal life remained active and the synagogue continued to be a focal point for local outside organisations. A request from the local branch of the Association of Jewish Ex-Serviceman (AJEX) to place their Branch Standard in the synagogue for six months was approved by the shul's Board of Management.[121] That spring, condolences were noted on the death of Mr. Eliash, the Israeli Minister in London, and also the passing of Paul Goodman, formerly chairman of the Synagogue Classes Committee.[122]

Complaints were registered again about conduct during services. Meeting in the Joseph Freedman Hall, the chairman implored the Board of Management to 'show on example of decorum as many [of them] talk too much during the Service.' New efforts were directed at forming a club for elderly members. It proved very popular and opened as the Friendship Club on 17 May, thanks to the hard work and dedication of Mrs Domb and the League of Jewish Women.

Changing the status of women in the congregation came to the fore too in April 1950 when Mr. Domb proposed the following resolution: 'That this Annual General Meeting for the Golders Green Synagogue calls on the Council of the United Synagogue to amend their Constitution, so that Lady Seatholders in their own right will have the power to vote at Synagogue elections in the future. It urges most strongly the immediate and serious consideration of this situation.' The resolution was carried.

Communal Life

In 1950, Rev. Livingstone reached the retirement age of 65, but requested an extension to his office as the minister. The Board unanimously passed a resolution: 'That Rev. I. Livingstone be granted one year's extension.' The Board would subsequently approve further extensions to his contract until 1953. Mendel Susser completed 25 years of service as Beadle to the Synagogue and all members received a letter asking to contribute one guinea towards the Presentation Fund for his retirement.

In May 1950, senior warden Alfred Woolf was elected Overseer of the Poor of the United Synagogue. Mr Barclay said at a meeting of the Board that: 'no man has proved himself more deserving of this great honour.' It was added to the Minutes that members of the Board expressed their 'gratification and deep sense of pride in his election.'

Cheder prize-giving with Rabbi Newman and Rev. Taschlicky. COURTESY: HELEN VEGODA

[121] Board of Management meeting, 19 February 1950.
[122] Board meeting on 30 April 1950.

High Holy Day services were as full as the previous decades and by 1951, such was the demand for seats that even the overflow services in the Joseph Freedman Hall were full to capacity. The hire of a local cinema or services in conjunction with Hendon Synagogue were amongst the suggestions made to resolve the situation.

The Hebrew and religion classes, under headmaster Mr. S. Kramer, aided by Rabbi Dr E. Lichtigfeld, numbered 141 boys and 85 girls, making a total membership of 226. The prize-giving for the children was held annually in March. In 1950, Rev. Myerovith replaced Rev. Epstein as the youth minister, and remained with congregation for a year. During 1950, a dance was arranged to raise funds for the classrooms. On the anniversary of a bar mitzvah, boys were called to the Reading Desk to read from the Torah. Alfred Woolf suggested that there should be special instruction of some kind for the girls, beyond the basic material for a Bat Mitzvah. It was acknowledged that the Chief Rabbi was already formulating a special curriculum for girls in the synagogues of the United Synagogue.

The Norwood Rat Club, raising money for the orphanage.

INVITATION
to the
ANNUAL DISTRIBUTION OF PRIZES

GOLDERS GREEN SYNAGOGUE
HEBREW AND RELIGION CLASSES

Headmaster - Mr. M. Ellman, B.A.

SUNDAY, 12th JUNE, 1966
at 11.45 a.m.

Guest of Honour: MR. S. KRAMER, B.A.

Distribution of Prizes by MRS. KRAMER.

In the Chair: MR. PHILIP COHEN
Chairman of the Education Committee

The Golders Green Jewish Youth Group, founded in 1943, was still going strong in the 1950s. Activities now included discussions, boxing, Modern Hebrew, music, badminton, rambles, socials, film shows and concert parties. The core aim of the group remained as a place where Jewish youth could meet each other 'in an atmosphere where they may develop a true sense of communal responsibility.'[123]

Dunstan Road had become a popular venue for weddings, with sometimes as many as four or five ceremonies a week. In addition, the serving minister undertook the bar mitzvahs and funerals. In 1950, Roy Caplan married Leah Ginsburg in the synagogue, the ceremony officiated by the bride's twin brothers, Rev. Alec Ginsburg and Rev. Sydney Ginsburg.[124] The *Jewish Chronicle* reported: 'They claim to be the only identical twin ministers in the Jewish faith, a claim that has not, so far, been contested.'[125]

Charitable Causes

The 1950s saw the continuation of the legendry annual *Gold & Green Ball*, in aid of charity, held at either the Savoy Hotel or Dorchester in Mayfair. The first one had been held in 1947 at the Savoy Hotel, an evening of dinner and dancing to Sydney Lipton and his ballroom orchestra. The *Gold & Green Ball* became a highlight of the year in the synagogue's social calendar. A brochure accompanied the event, and local businesses could pay for an advertisement at 30 guineas for a full page and 17 guineas a half page, and the proceeds donated to the chosen charities. 'Our parents worked tirelessly to organise the event,' comments Winston Newman. 'There was always a large tombola for

---

[123] Letter to members, dated 20 April 1951, amongst the club's papers, lent to the author by Jeremy Manuel.

[124] At that time, Rev. Sydney Ginsburg was junior Minister at the Southend and Westcliffe Hebrew Congregation. Rev. Alec Ginsburg was Senior Jewish Chaplain to the British Army of the Rhine. Rev. Alec Ginsburg went on to become Rabbi of Plymouth Hebrew Congregation. Roy and Leah Caplan are buried at the Gifford Place Jewish Cemetery in Plymouth.

[125] Information supplied by Dr Rob Ginsburg, son of Rev. Alec Ginsburg. Dr Ginsburg is today on the Board of Management of the shul and he and his family are long time members of the shul.

GOLDERS GREEN JOINT CHARITIES COMMITTEE

SEVENTH MAMMOTH BAZAAR

to be held on

Sunday & Monday
13th and 14th December, 1953

from 2 p.m. till 10 p.m., at

THE JOSEPH FREEDMAN HALL
Dunstan Road, N.W.11

*In the past six years more than £18,000 has been distributed
to the following causes amongst others:*

**Central British Fund   Home & Hospital for Jewish Incurables   Jewish Blind Society
Jewish Board of Guardians**

**Kosher School Meals Service   Jewish Child's Day   Chevra Bikur Cholim
Friends of the Hebrew University   The Orde Wingate Children's Village
Bachad Fellowship   The Jewish Friendship Clubs   Home for Aged Jews
Jewish National Fund Commission   Anti-Tuberculosis League for Israel**

EVERYTHING of EVERY KIND for EVERY OCCASION

Enquiries and Gifts to:

Joint Hon. Organisers:
   Mrs. L. M. FREEDEN, c/o 237 Baker Street, N.W.1. WEL. 0293
   Miss Nancy HURSTBOURNE, c/o Woburn House,
                          Upper Woburn Place, W.C.1 EUS. 6869

Hon. Secretary:
   Mr. H. S. WARD, Joseph Freedman Hall, Dunstan Road, N.W.11. SPE 2460

★ ORDER FORM OVERLEAF

Bertha Newman and ladies of the synagogue, charity fundraising at tombola stall, 1950s.

the event, and the tombola goods were stored in their house for many months before the Ball, rendering their lounge unusable during this period.

From the late 1950s, the Golders Green Combined Charities Committee hosted, what became known as, the *Gold and Green Champagne Dinner and Ball* at the Dorchester Hotel in Park Lane. It was quite an occasion with dancing to van Straten and his orchestra until 1am in the morning. The host and hostess were Mr & Mrs Frankie Vaughan. Unlike today, mixed dancing was very much a feature of United Synagogue events.

The congregation remained active in organising many other charitable events, including the annual Mammoth Bazaar in the Joseph Freedman Hall. In 1951, the charities who benefitted from this event were Orde Wingate Children's Village, the Friends of the Hebrew University, Jewish Child's Day and Homes for Aged Jews. Prizes were donated for a draw on the second day of the event, prizes such as a television set (an expensive commodity in the 1950s), bottles of whisky, gramophone records and nylon stockings. An accompanying brochure with paid advertisements raised funds for the charities, too. In the six years up to 1953, the bazaar raised a total of £18,000, distributed amongst a number of charitable causes that included the Jewish Blind Society, Kosher School Meals Service, The Central British Fund, the Joint Palestine Appeal, the Home for Aged Jews, Jewish Board of Guardians, and Home & Hospital for Jewish Incurables.

Appointment of Rabbi Newman

The congregation's Minute Book reveal that no fewer than fifteen ministers were vying for the post to succeed Rev. Livingstone. Three applicants made the final shortlist.[126] The Board of Management offered the post to Rev. Dr Barnett Joseph who was the minister of Sheffield at that time. Rev. Dr Barnett's successful appointment was reported to his congregation, as he awaited ratification by the membership of Golders Green Synagogue. That was somewhat premature because, in a surprise move, his appointment was rejected by the synagogue membership at a General Meeting. The post had to be re-advertised and Rabbi Newman was appointed with the full backing of the congregation.

Rabbi Newman's induction took place on 23 March 1954, officiated by Chief Rabbi Israel Brodie and attended by over a thousand people. Also present at the induction were Rev. Isaac Levy of Hampstead Synagogue, Dr W. Van der Zyl of the North-Western Reform Synagogue, Alyth Gardens and representatives of the United Synagogue. In an address to his new congregation, Rabbi Newman outlined his vision for the youth of the community and said: 'My plan is to teach the traditional Judaism on which the synagogue is based. Teaching it to the younger generation is the greatest safeguard for its continuity and survival.' The service was followed by a reception in the Joseph Freedman Hall.

---

[126] They were Rabbi Eugene Newman, Rabbi Isaac Chait and Rev. Dr Barnett Joseph.

Induction of Rabbi Newman, March 1954. Seated front row, l to r: Jimmy Seaford, Barnet Beckman, Rev. Livingstone, Rabbi Newman, Rev. Taschlicky, Myer Harris, Alfred Woolf. Standing back row, l to r: Harry Ward, Arthur Taylor, Seymour Craig, Mr S. London, Morris Laufer, David Manuel, Maurice Domb, Mr Haltrecht, Harry Wasser, Mr Lange, Mr Keene, Sidney Ellis, Jacob Greenbaum, Judah Blackman.

With a background in the strictly orthodox communities of pre-war Europe, Rabbi Newman, brought a different dimension to the religious atmosphere at the Dunstan Road shul at a time when the membership had already begun to decline. The synagogue had enjoyed an unrivalled large membership as the only purpose-built shul in the immediate vicinity for almost two decades, but now its membership was in decline, in part due to the number of alternative communities in the area, both orthodox and reform. Rabbi Dr Newman sought to attract new members, to make the shul a place where members felt at home, regardless of their level of observance. Membership totalled around 854 male members, 155 female members and 140 assessed members. Wives who applied to become members in their own right were able to vote at Annual Meetings.

Rabbi Newman faced his own challenge in keeping the community vibrant because, as he himself once commented: 'one of the big problems in this area is the lack of purpose-built flats. Many of the couples who have moved away have said they would prefer to remain here, but have found it impossible to find suitable homes.'

'He was a very good pastoral Rabbi,' comments Brian Beckman. 'The shul began to change character with the reintroduction of youth services. He introduced weekly Talmud and Bible lessons which had fallen into decline before he arrived.'

Rabbi Newman's wife, Bertha, was also very active in the community. Her daughter, Adele, recalls: 'The Ladies' Guild lunches, with my mother as chairman, were always very popular events and with well-known speakers. The prolific novelist and great character, Barbara Cartland, was a frequent speaker. Mum used to describe how her chauffeur would bring her Rolls Royce right up to the door of the Joseph Freedman Hall. Another regular speaker was well known actress Bettine le Beau.'

Bertha Newman organised the local Poppy Day appeal for the Golders Green area. Their home was the main centre for the poppy trays and collecting boxes, and a communal focal point for meetings, counselling and friendship. For many years, Mrs Newman was chairman of the Ladies' Association which met regularly and raised money for the shul and charities from coffee mornings and bazaars. She supported Emunah (formerly Women's Mizrachi) from its inception in Manchester in the 1940s, and despite her full-time activities for the Golders Green Synagogue, which she enjoyed so much, she continued her support of Emunah throughout her life. She remembered chairing an unremarkable luncheon at which the guest speaker was Mrs Thatcher (later, the first female British Prime Minister).

After the first year in post, Rabbi Newman was described as having 'carried out his duties with the greatest devotion and zeal and has not spared himself in the service

THE GOLDERS GREEN FRIENDSHIP CLUB

Meets every Wednesday at 2.30 p.m. at the Golders Green Synagogue Hall, Dunstan Road, N.W.11.

Committee Meetings are held on the first Wednesday of each month at the Synagogue Hall, at 1.0 p.m. unless otherwise notified.

Hon. Sec.:
Mrs. Eve Laurence,
II9 Hendon Way,
N.W.2   SPE 5702

work of the youth was supported by financial assistance and donations of books from members of the shul, often in memory of a relative. Well-attended children's services were held every Shabbat and Festival mornings in the Joseph Freedman Hall, officiated by Mr J. Weinstock, assisted by Ruth Halpern. The monthly youth service for teenagers over the age of 13 had become a regular part of synagogue life.

On 26 September 1954, the synagogue's War Memorial was unveiled in the vestibule by Alderman Bernard Waley Cohen, a Vice-President of the United Synagogue. The Minutes record: 'An impressive Memorial in the form of a tablet containing the names of relatives of members of the congregation who gave their lives in the First and Second World Wars, together with a fountain, was erected in the vestibule of the synagogue.'

Financed by the generosity of Norman Bloom, in memory of his parents and Mrs Bloom's father, it was consecrated by the Senior Jewish Chaplain to the forces, Rev. Isaac Levy OBE, together with the ministers of the synagogue. The Association of Jewish Ex-Servicemen and Women provided standard bearers and trumpeters of the Royal Horse Guards.

Mrs Bertha Newman speaking at one of the many luncheons at the synagogue. COURTESY THE NEWMAN FAMILY

At the Shabbat morning service on 19 March 1955, two marble tablets containing the Prayer for the State of Israel, one in Hebrew, the other in English, were consecrated. They were donated by a member of the congregation who wished to remain anonymous. A library was established in the Board Room for the benefit of the community, with book donations from Mr W. Behr, Israel Cohen, Mr M. Domb, Jacob Greenbaum, Mr J. Landau, Mr B. Levy, Mr J. Millett, Mr M. Myers, Mr L. Schoenfeld and Mr H. Wasser.

From the mid 1950s, children's Shabbat services resumed under the direction of Mr J. Weinstock as honorary officiant, assisted by Ruth Halpern. A monthly youth service is held for boys and girls over the age of 13, conducted entirely by the boys themselves. Alfred Woolf JP, chaired the newly formed Parents' Association with

of the congregation.'[127] As promised in his induction speech, he introduced many activities, especially for the children and youth of the congregation which 'proved to be of the greatest benefit to the spiritual welfare of the congregation.'

Rabbi Newman led The Study Circle, and also the Junior Study Circle on Shabbat afternoons, and Senior Study Circle on Friday evenings in people's homes. His first year as minister also saw a welcome visit to the synagogue by Chief Rabbi Israel Brodie. Rabbi Newman was ably assisted in services and communal occasions by the Emeritus Minister, Rev. Livingstone who was given a special seat in the synagogue. Rev. Taschlicky continued, too, to conduct services in his 'excellent manner'. The beadle, Mendel Susser, reached the age of 65 and, much to the regret of the congregation, offered his retirement. It was noted that: 'his efficiency, tact and knowledge of the members of the congregation, has always been of great assistance in the smooth running of the congregation.'

By the mid 1950s, numbers in Hebrew classes had risen from 226 to 296, of whom 112 were girls. The rise in attendance necessitated nine separate classes. The children took part in the annual competitive examinations of the London Board of Jewish Religious Education, and Golders Green achieved a 100 per cent success rate. The education

---

[127] The Annual Report for 1954/5.

attended to matters of children's welfare, religion classes, and additional youth activities. It sponsored new prayer books for use during Children's Services.

The Joint Palestine Appeal for the year 1954/5 raised £3,000 during Kol Nidre. The total sum raised for various charities amounted to £9,000. The sum of £7,350 was raised for Jews' College, thanks to the energetic efforts and leadership of Mr M. Laufer.

The Golders Green Friendship Club, which boasted around 200 members over the age of 60, continue to be strong and met every Wednesday afternoon in the Joseph Freedman Hall. The hall was also used by external Jewish organizations: Jewish Youth Study Groups, Habonim, Ezra Youth Organisation, various Zionist groups and the Jewish Blind Society, and for receptions after weddings and bar mitzvahs.

From the mid 1950s

For the twelve months of 1955-56, total membership of the synagogue stood at 1,150, of which 180 were women. The children's religion school received a record membership of 321, of which 210 were boys and 111 girls. The finances of the synagogue looked healthy with a record income of £20,000. The choir continued to enhance services under the leadership of David Levine. Visiting minsters during this period included Rabbi Dr I. S. Rosenberg of Jerusalem and Rabbi Mordecai Kirschblum of New York. Mendel Susser agreed to continue as Beadle for a further year until a suitable replacement could be found. The congregation mourned the passing of two distinguished members: past Senior Warden Barnet Beckman whose 'scholarship and innate modesty endeared him to his colleagues, his death leaving 'a void in our community and his memory will long be cherished.' Also, the passing of Professor Samson Wright, a member of the synagogue for many years and distinguished figure in Anglo-Jewry, and the world of medicine.

The Cultural and Literary Society remained active, members paying a nominal subscription of 5s. per annum, with a membership of almost 300. Activities included many lectures, one for example, by Rabbi Dr S. Gaon on *The Contributions of the Sephardim to Jewish Life*. The Kosher Cookery Classes, held in the precincts of the synagogue, remained one of the most popular groups. The cultural events included securing internationally-acclaimed people like British concert pianist Harriet Cohen and physicist Professor Samuels Tolansky, the latter nominated for a Nobel Prize for his investigations into the optical characteristics of moon dust from the Apollo 11 moon landing. Israeli films were screened at other meetings and a series of debates held on whether the State of Israel should

be incorporated into the British Commonwealth of Nations.

In 1955, the Ladies' Society celebrated forty years of activity since its formation in 1915 with a special tea to mark the occasion. Mrs Livingstone gave a summary of their activities over the four decades and past members living in other parts of London were invited. The first chairwoman, Lady Benjamin Drage, sent a beautiful cake. Throughout the year, the Ladies' Society organised numerous teas, with a visit to the Tercentenary Exhibition at the V&A Museum. Garments were made for good causes, in this year being sent to the Highbury Home and the London Jewish Hospital.

The synagogue was justly proud to have distributed over £20,000 to various charities over an 8-year period.

The Swinging Sixties

By now, the congregation comprised mainly second-generation membership from the families who had originally started the congregation back in 1915. It was very 'London, English,' comments Alan Mays whose family moved to Golders Green circa 1959. 'There were some Holocaust survivors amongst the congregants, but most survivors in the area attended the Munk's Synagogue. Some memories stay with you, like the Sunday trading laws at that time which meant that only Jewish shops were open on a Sunday: the hardware stores, bakeries and delicatessens. I remember the queues for Cohen's smoked salmon.'[128]

Golders Green Synagogue remained one of the most popular and fashionable venues for marriages. Jewish families, too, were moving out of the East End and Willesden to relocate to smart Golders Green and Hendon because it was not far from the countryside of Hampstead Heath and leafy Garden Suburb. Amongst the congregants was Rev. Joseph Halpern, an international Biblical scholar, given the honorary title because of his learning.

Services were still 'high church', conducted by officials in canonicals. Alan Mays, recalls the busy attendance on High Holy days: 'I used to sit on a step near my father for the High Holy Day services because there wasn't a single seat to be had in the shul. It was very atmospheric. There were over a thousand people in the main synagogue. We had overflow services to accommodate members who only came two or three times a year. The majority of congregants in this period came, not necessarily for the learning, but because of the services – they came to hear the cantor, Rev. Taschlicky who had a magnificent dramatic voice, and the professional choir.'

The choir consisted of professional singers under lead singer, Martin Lawrence.[129] Rev. Taschlicky aided Rabbi

---

[128] Alan Mays in interview with the author, 2015.

[129] Originally Charles Schloss from the East End. He was a Communist who travelled to Russia and China. Because of his views, he couldn't secure a job at Sadler's Wells or in Covent Garden.

Golda Meir and Moshe Sharett (seated). With from left to right standing: Aaron Wright, Charles Barclay, Alfred Woolf and David Manuel.

Opening of the Lebetkin hall. From left to right: Chief Rabbi Israel Brodie, Mr Lou Lebetkin, Rabbi Newman and Rev. Taschlicky.

Newman with hospital visits and Shivas. Rabbi Newman ran a daily Shiur after weekday morning services which was well received. The headmaster of the Hebrew and Religion Classes was now Mr M. Ellman.

The Minute Books again shed light on the day-to-day issues facing the community. In January 1961, the Board of Management received a letter from the United Synagogue informing them that it was not legal to have gaming machines on the premises, and this must be raised with the various organisations who rented the premises.[130] Plans were discussed to extend the kitchen at a cost of £900, of which the United Synagogue had offered to pay half. A donation of £100 was given by the Kosher Cooking Classes who would benefit most from the improvements. A generous donation for this was also received from Mr. M. Lange on the occasion of the wedding of his son Freddie to Tessa Schana and to commemorate 25 years of joining the Synagogue. From the third week of February 1961, redecoration of the synagogue was carried out in an entirely new colour scheme of three shades of blue, gold and cream. The renovations took three weeks and, in liaison, with the architect, it was decided to paint the ceiling a light sky blue and the walls a darker blue. The use of blue as the predominate colour was, according to Rabbi Newman, 'a traditional Jewish colour.' Instead of black, the pillars were painted a warm stone and the bases and indentations pitched out in gold. The woodwork and Ark were treated and stained, and the vestibule painted a stone colour. That autumn, the cost of seat rental for members rose for the first time in ages and ranged from £8.10 to £35 for the best seats. The following was noted in detail in Minutes and provides an interesting piece of communal social history:

Men's Seats

Row A	40 seats	From £30.10.4 to £35.0.0
Row B	42 seats	From £25.0.6 to £29.0.0
Row C	32 seats	From £22.6.6 to £26.0.0
Row D	91 seats	From £19.11.6 to £23.0.0
Row E	140 seats	From £16.17.0 to £20.0.0
Row F	151 seats	From £13.10.0 to £17.0.0
Row G	44 seats	From £11.19.2 to £15.0.0
Row H	58 seats	From £10.11.6 to £13.0.0
Row I	20 seats	From £8.10.0 to £10.0.0

Ladies Seats

Row A	92 seats	From £8.3.10 to £10.0.0
Row B	80 seats	From £6.16.10 to £8.0.0
Row C	104 seats	From £5.9.6 to £6.10.0
Row D	97 seats	From £4.2.0 to £5.0.0
Row E	14 seats	From £2.14.0 to £3.10.0

The rise in rent brought in an increased income of £3,000 a year, which would aid the synagogue's increased expenditure and overheads. Of course, no decade would be complete without mention of decorum during services. It was noted:

'The question of decorum and particularly of members and visitors being called up for an Aliyah and wearing Koppuls and not hats, was giving the Honorary Officers much concern. They would suggest to the Board that a small label should be affixed to Yahrzeit notices that went out to members drawing their attention to the fact that it was the custom of this synagogue for the person being called to the Reading of the Law to wear a hat.'[131]

From left to right: Harry Ward, Rabbi Newman and Rev. Taschlicky, 1960s

At one meeting of the Board of Management, Mr Cowan drew attention to an accident on the corner of Hodford Road and Dunstan Road in which a young member of one of the synagogue clubs was killed on his motorbike. It was agreed to raise the danger of this corner with Hendon Borough Council. The situation was subsequently the subject of serious discussion within the Council's Highway Committee and Ministry of Transport and a decision was taken to erect a *Halt* sign at the junction, and also a sign near the synagogue, *Dead Slow Children*.[132]

In 1965, Rev. Taschlicky completed 30 years of dedicated service to the shul. Alfred Woolf JP led the delegation which had gone to Israel to interview the Chief Rabbi elect, Dr. J. Hertzog.[133] That same year, the synagogue's finances had a net surplus of £339, of which £200 was required to supplement the costs of the official choir.

After an alarming arson attack on Brondesbury Synagogue during the 1960s, the security of synagogues became a matter of paramount importance. Rabbi Newman was involved in the early days of keeping watch and

---

[130] There is no information given in the Minutes about which organisations used gaming machines.
[131] Meeting, 21 June 1962.
[132] Meeting held on 3 September 1964.
[133] May 1965.

preparing defensive measures through the night. Concern was again raised in November 1965 over fire safety of the synagogue on Guy Fawkes Night, and also 9/10 November – the anniversary of Kristallnacht. On these nights, the synagogue and premises were guarded by nearby neighbours and volunteers from the shul's Parents' Association.

The current Ark in the shul was found to be insufficient to house all the Sefrei Torah. A decision was taken to engage an architect to draw up plans for an enlarged Ark that would also be fire-proof, a lesson learned after the fire at Brondesbury Synagogue. It was added to the Minutes

that the two Leder brothers were willing to donate £1,000 towards the cost.[134]

A number of items were donated to the synagogue, including a velvet Ark curtain from Mr and Mrs Berg on the bar mitzvah of their twin sons, Robert and Alan; two Sedra Boards on the bar mitzvah of Laurence Stephen Brass, donated by his parents Mr and Mrs S. Brass; a Sefer Torah and mantle from Mr S. Heinrich in memory of his wife, Rosa, and dedicated on 11 December 1960; and a yad for a Sefer Torah by Rev. Taschlicky on the occasion of his 25 years' service to the congregation.

Charitable Causes

During 1961-62, the Golders Green Combined Charities Committee had helped 78 charities and raised a total of £4,050.[135] Amongst the beneficiaries were the Whittington Hospital, Club for the Physically handicapped, Variety

Dr Vivian Lipman.

The ambulance donated by the community to Magen David Adom.
COURTESY:
MICHAEL JOLLES

---

[134] Entry in Minute Book, 7 November 1966.
[135] Reported by Mr. Domb at a meeting on 7 March 1962.

Jackie Crossley and with mother Leila.

Artists Benevolent Fund, Mifal Hatorah Medical Aid Fund, Yeshiva Etz Chaim Breakfast Fund, Stamford Hill Talmud Torah and Merkaz Yeshivot Bnei Akiva in Tev Aviv, Israel, Jews' College, Residential School for the Deaf, AJEX, Hendon Mayor's Fund for Old People, Kosher Meal Service, Polio Research Fund, Dr Barnardos Homes, Stepney Boys Club, and many more.

The *Gold and Green Ball*, held at the Dorchester on Valentine's Day 1961, raised a total of £5,500. It enabled the congregation to purchase an ambulance for Magen David Adom, to be sent to Israel. The Minute Book noted: 'The generosity in particular of Mr and Mrs Michael Wix, associated with the shul since it first opened in 1915, meant that the community exceeded its financial target for charitable causes this year.' The ambulance was formally handed over to Magen David Adom at a special Service of Dedication on 19 March, conducted by Rabbi Newman, Rev. Livingstone and Rev. Taschlicky. Helen Bentwich unveiled it, and her husband, Norman Bentwich OBE, gave the presentation. Vice-Chairman Norman Joseph formally accepted the ambulance on behalf of the Friends of Magen David Adom.

During the 1960s, Mr M. Domb and Dr S. Torrance acted as wardens for the overflow services on High Holy Days which continued to be held in the Joseph Freedman Hall. The Parents' Association of the shul supported the

vital Kosher School Meals Service, the Hebrew classes and Youth Club. The roll call for religion classes had reached a high of 270 and monthly youth services were well attended.

The synagogue occasionally received visits from non-Jewish theological students. Rabbi Newman was also keen to address other Christian groups about Judaism. This period also saw the formation of the South Hendon branch of the Council of Christians and Jews.

Of all the controversies in the synagogue's hundred-year history, the issue of installing a central bimah dragged on for over a decade and was one in which opinion was divided. The matter features quite prominently in the Minute Books from 1966. At a meeting of the Board of Management on 25 January 1966, Mr P. Cohen who was chairing, commented that the shul was one of the few Orthodox synagogues not to have a central bimah. He asked Board members to consider whether to take this idea further and engage an architect to draw up plans. It was agreed to explore the idea, but to have no formal agreement that it would definitely happen. Rabbi Newman himself supported the idea of a central bimah.

Two months later, the Board discussed the arguments for and against a central bimah, resulting in the meeting ending 'at a late hour' and decision postponed until a later date.[136] At the Annual General Meeting on 12 May 1968, the following resolution was passed:

'That this Annual General Meeting of Members requests and authorises the Board of Management to make all necessary enquiries relevant to the erection of a bimah in the centre of the synagogue, and to report back their findings to a Special Meeting of Members for this decision.'

The hope that this matter could be resolved in the near future would soon be dashed. The argument about a central bimah was to dominate much of the next decade until its resolution in 1978.

Rabbi Newman preparing a boy for his bar mitzvah.

CHAPTER 8

Transition and Change

THE 1970S MARKED a time of transition and change for a congregation that would see the sudden death of its beloved Rabbi, Dr Eugene Newman whilst still in post, a celebration of the Golden Jubilee of the building, the appointment of Rabbi Jonathan Sacks who would later become Chief Rabbi of the United Hebrew Congregations of the Commonwealth and a highly respected public figure, and the death of its first permanent minister, Rev. Livingstone.

The congregation still had a full time secretary and chazan. Membership was large enough to continue one or two overflow services for High Holy Days and other major festivals. A voluntary community choir was formed, led by

Alan Mays. He recalls: 'With 6 or 7 members, it was a much less formal choir and brought a fresh approach. We sat at the side of the Ark, rather than in the choir stall and revived old tunes to inspire people to join in the singing during the services.' Daniel Greenberg, son of Gillian and Morris Greenberg, recalled his childhood growing up in the 1970s and described the community as: 'a wonderful place for Jewish boys to develop and find their own place in Judaism.' He found himself 'surrounded by a wealth of personalities and opportunities.'[137] Even so, numbers in religion school were already falling, with only 12-20 children attending the weekday classes.

During the 1970s, three long-standing members of the

Induction of Rev. Meir Finkelstein, November 1971. COURTESY: MAURICE SAMUELSON

---

[137] The GGS Journal, September 2012.

Alfred Woolf, OBE.

Golders Green Synagogue were honoured by the Queen. David Gedalla was appointed MBE in recognition of his services as Secretary of the Jews' Temporary Shelter. In 1975, Alfred Woolf, one-time President of the United Synagogue, was appointed OBE. Woolf served the United Synagogue as Treasurer of Bequests & Trusts from 1950-59, Treasurer from 1959-61, Vice President 1961-1973, and President 1973 – 1977. Nathan Reuben, Secretary of the United Synagogue, was honoured by the Queen with the award of the Silver Jubilee Medal in recognition of his work in many field but primarily in education.

In 1970, Rev. Meir Finkelstein was inaugurated as the youngest cantor to be appointed to the Golders Green Synagogue. He led the formal choir of the congregation, having studied at the Royal College of Music. Only 18 years old when he arrived, he brought a lighter touch when he took over from Rev. Taschlicky after the latter's retirement. His services were appreciated such that the Minute Book later recorded that: 'The Rev. Meir Finkelstein has continued to delight us with his chazanuth. He is continuing his musical studies at the Royal College of Music with excellent reports of his progress.'[138]

On 4 April 1971, a Sefer Torah donated by the family of the late Myer Kaizer and Arthur Kaizer was consecrated in the synagogue by Rabbi Newman and Rev. Finkelstein, also a Parochot for the Ark from Mr & Mrs Jack Bogush in memory of their parents, and a cover for the Reading Desk

Consecration of a Torah scroll in memory of Mrs Annie Bell, November 1971.

[138] Entry in the Minute Book summary in 1972.

Centre of Golders Green 1970s. COURTESY: HENDON LIBRARY & ARCHIVES

Golders Green Road 1970s. COURTESY: HENDON LIBRARY & ARCHIVES

presented by Mr & Mrs Eric Davis in memory of their parents.

The synagogue committees had always provided a vital role in the running of the community. Amongst them were the Classes Committee, Choir and Services Committee, Youth Committee, Membership and Finance Committee, working alongside the Board of Management. Representatives from Golders Green Synagogue were elected to various United Synagogue Committees: Bequests and Trusts Committee, Building Committee, and Burial Committee. A representative was also sent to Board of Deputies meetings.

In 1972, Rabbi Newman was appointed a member of the Chief Rabbi's Cabinet in charge of Welfare. It was also the year that his doctoral thesis (conferred in 1968) was published and the year in which his eldest son, Michael, received *Semicha*. Michael was 7-years-old when his father was appointed minister of the synagogue. The congregation 'watched and followed his brilliant career through school, Jews' College and University College, London, and finally in a Yeshiva in Israel, from which he received *Semicha* from the most eminent Rabbis in that country. We congratulate him and his family sincerely and heartily and wish him well in his chosen career.'

Later that same year, a new Beadle, Mr. B. Taite, took up post at the synagogue.[139] Work began, too, on the redecoration of the synagogue, during which time Shabbat services were held in the Joseph Freedman Hall. Philip Shaw submitted a new lighting scheme for the synagogue which was in urgent need of electrical work. Donations of £1,000 were received towards the project, estimated to cost £3,800. By August 1972, redecoration of the shul was almost complete and the new lighting to be installed by Messrs. Focus Lighting. The Minute Book noted later that year that: 'The appearance and décor of the Synagogue were notably improved during the year by its complete redecoration and by renewal of the lighting fittings. The redecoration, for which we have to thank the United Synagogue, was planned by a colour expert and the final result was, as far as we can judge, generally approved. The lighting scheme was the separate responsibility of the community and we are most grateful to those members who contributed to the cost.'

The United Synagogue sent a letter to all is constituent synagogues, urging them to support the Jewish National Fund Forest as a tribute to the Queen and Duke of Edinburgh on their Silver Wedding in 1972.

The Synagogue's Golden Jubilee Year

The fiftieth anniversary of the consecration of the synagogue was marked in 1972 by 'a number of memorable and pleasurable events.' Amongst those events was an

Rabbi Newman, civic ceremony at the synagogue with Chief Rabbi Immanuel Jakobovits, 1970s.

[139] He took up the position from November 1972.

enjoyable concert in the Joseph Freedman Hall on 19 March by the Zemel Choir and the congregation's Chazan, the Rev. Meir Finkelstein. A week earlier, Emeritus minister Rev. Livingstone delivered a lecture to the Cultural and Literary Society about the previous fifty-year history of the synagogue. It was noted that 'those present found Mr. Livingstone's fund of memories of those early days extremely interesting.'

Two major events marked the Jubilee – a special Banquet and Ball, and a Jubilee Service. The banquet was held in the King David Suite on 21 November, attended by around 240 people, all of whom 'thoroughly enjoyed and appreciated the pleasant family atmosphere of this happy occasion.' Addressing the function were Rabbi Newman, Rev. Livingstone and Alfred Woolf, J.P., the latter in his dual capacity as a member of the Golders Green Synagogue for well over 40 years and its senior warden, and as the Senior Vice-President of the United Synagogue.

Party for Rat boxes (charity event), held in the Joseph Freedman Hall.

At 3 p.m. on Sunday 26 November, a Jubilee Service was held, to which over a hundred VIPs had been invited. The service was attended by approximately 500 people, including a large number of visitors from other synagogues and local churches, as well as several local dignitaries: the Mayor of Barnet, Alderman J. L. Freedman and the Mayoress, Councillor Mrs. Freedman, and the Rt. Hon Peter Thomas, Q.C., M.P., Minister of State for Wales and Member of Parliament for the constituency. Officiating clergy were the Chief Rabbi Immanuel Jakobovits, Rabbi Newman, Rev. Finkelstein, Rev. Livingstone, and Rev. Taschlicky. The choir was led by Jack Cohen. In his address, Chief Rabbi Immanuel Jakobovits quoted from Dr. Hertz's corresponding address during the original Consecration Service of 1922 and observed how appropriate much of it was to the present occasion. He also made clear his own special high regard for the synagogue and spoke of the wealth of communal activity engendered from it. A reception tea followed in the Harris Lebetkin Hall.

The Ladies' Association marked the Jubilee year by donating a library to the synagogue, library consecrated on

25 March. Rabbi Newman told the congregation: 'Now we have celebrated the Jubilee of our synagogue may each of us resolve to make his and her contribution to its various activities so that our synagogue may continue to be a leading religious and spiritual force in the area.'

There were other reasons to celebrate during the synagogue's jubilee. The community joined in celebrations relating to some of its most respected members. These included the Diamond Wedding anniversary of the Rev. and Mrs. Livingstone, and the Golden Wedding anniversaries of Mr and Mrs Alfred Woolf and Mr and Mrs Sam Mitzman. It was noted: 'Our Emeritus Minister and his wife, after 60 happy years of marriage, by some miracle, have retained the youth and charm which made such an impression at his appointment to Golders Green 58 years ago.' Of Mr. and Mrs. Sam Mitzman, mention was made that they had been 'members of our community for over half of their married life and, with their children and grandchildren, are still most active in every way. Our very heartiest congratulations go to this most popular set of brides and grooms.'

There were celebrations, too, for Daisy and Alfred Woolf who had moved to Golders Green forty-four years earlier and had served the community throughout this period 'in an exemplary manner,' combining his duties for the Golders Green Synagogue and United Synagogue alongside the task of being a local Magistrate.

From left to right: Rev. Taschlicky, Harry Ward, A. Guy Walker, and Mr Philip.

Central Bimah

The issue of a central bimah came to the fore in the 1970s, almost a decade after it was first raised in a meeting of the Board of Management. The Central Bimah Committee was formed, initially chaired by Philip Cohen. Elected to it were Mr. S. Boder, Michael Martin, Michael Mays, Mr. S. Palace and Mr. M. Rose. Thus far, although there was a general consensus to proceed with a central bimah, Mr Lerner pointed out to the Board that, apart from a verbal statement from Mr. Rubin (Secretary of the United

The Lebetkin Hall

Synagogue), there was nothing in writing to say that they could go ahead. It was not until January 1973 that the Board received a letter which stated that the synagogue could proceed with the *proposal* to erect a central bimah. This was subject to conditions:-

1. That detailed plans are submitted for approval by the Building Committee (of the United Synagogue). These plans will also have to indicate any alterations that are to be made in the existing seating and synagogue as a consequent of the Building of the Centre Bimah.

2. That the whole of the cost of erecting the Centre Bimah, consequential alterations and professional fees, be met entirely from local funds and that the amount be deposited with the United Synagogue immediately prior to the commencement of the work.

Plans submitted to Building Committee of the United Synagogue were finally approved, with an estimated cost of £3,000 to £4,000. The family of Martin Geminder had offered to defray the cost of the project up to a maximum of £5,000 on a seven-year covenant. In spite of approving the plans, the United Synagogue made a suggestion that the Golders Green Synagogue use the bimah from Brondesbury Synagogue which had closed in 1974, its members transferring to the congregation renamed the

A day in the shul office. From the left: Simon Rurka, Judah Blackman, Harry Ward. COURTESY: HELEN VEGODA

Willesden and Brondesbury Synagogue.[140] An entry in the Minute Book for 9 October 1975 notes a resolution that: 'this Board of Management authorises the co-chairmen of the Bimah Committee, Michael Mays and Mr. S. Palace, to take up with those concerned at the Head Office of the United Synagogue the question of the whereabouts of the Brondesbury bimah.' Confusion emerged because it was not clear what had happened to the bimah from Brondesbury and it was understood that it had been moved to the Willesden Synagogue.

---

[140] Bernard Susser, *The History of the Willesden and Brondesbury Synagogue, 1934-1994.*

From the mid 1970s

Overflow services in the Joseph Freedman Hall for the High Holy Day services in the autumn of 1973 were poorly attended, with only three quarters of the seats taken. The roll call for children's *cheder* on a Sunday was now sixty-five with six classes. In contrast, the Youth Club had a membership of two hundred and twenty. Elected to the Choir and Services Committee in this period were Brian Beckman, Sidney Boder, Dr Arnold Cohen, Mr M. Jacobs, Michael Mays, Alan Mays, Sam Mitzman, Sidney Palace, David Shapiro, Mr H. Wasser and Dr Ernest Woolf.

The Woolf family: Anthony, Alfred, Barbara and Daisy.

On 1 June 1975, Rev. Chaim Abramovitz was appointed the new Reader after the resignation of Rev. Finkelstein to take up a new post. An inscribed Kiddish cup and tray was given to him on his leaving, in appreciation of his services to the community. Rev. Chaim Abramovitz took on hospital visits and visits to mourners, as well as regularly participating in morning and evening services. He was described as 'an inspiration,' and his support was great appreciated by Rabbi Newman. Born in Lodz, Poland, Rev. Abramovitz studied at a Yeshiva in Rishon-le-Zion where his parents had moved with their family. At the age of sixteen, he served in the Israeli Army in the war of 1948. From 1960-61, he moved to Peru where he became cantor at the Sharon Synagogue in Lima, and then at the Shaarei Tsedek Congregation in Curcacao from 1961-64. In 1967, he came to England as Reader at the Beth Hamedrash Hagadol in Leeds. He was inducted as Reader at Golders Green Synagogue on 30 August 1975, serving the congregation until appointment to St John's Wood Synagogue in 1982.[141]

During 1975, Alfred Woolf was re-elected as President of the United Synagogue and Rev. Livingstone was appointed Emeritus Minister of the United Synagogue. Congratulations were sent to Soloman Martin on reaching his 100th birthday. The following year, Harry Ward and his wife were presented with a tea set for their Ruby Wedding.

Already, the congregation was struggling to gather enough men for *Mincha* (afternoon) and Ma'ariv (evening) services. Attendance at Shabbat morning services began to

fall in the coming years, such that letters were sent out to members to encourage them to attend regularly. By 1977, the community struggled to maintain three religion classes during the winter months. In spite of this decline in attendance, membership itself remained fairly static and the community was active with its regular clubs: the Golders Green Friendship Club, the Cultural and Literary Society and the various Ladies' groups. The Ladies' Society met regularly to make up parcels of fruit, sweets, chocolates and cigarettes for patients in various mental hospitals. A group of patients from Napsbury Mental Home were given

United Synagogue—ק״ק כנסת ישראל
GOLDERS GREEN SYNAGOGUE
HEBREW AND RELIGION CLASSES
Dunstan Road, N.W.11

You are cordially invited to attend the

ANNUAL PRIZE DISTRIBUTION

to be held at the
JOSEPH FREEDMAN HALL
on SUNDAY, JUNE 4th, 1972 at 11 a.m.

Guest of Honour : MR. ASHER FISHMAN, LL.B.
Chairman of the London Board of Jewish Religious Education

DISTRIBUTION OF PRIZES by MRS. FISHMAN

---

[141] I am grateful to Michael Jolles for this biographical material, supplied from his vast array of research for a book on British Jewish Cantors.

Temple Fortune shops. COURTESY: HENDON LIBRARY & ARCHIVES

a fish tea and entertainment, with help from children of the Pardes House Primary School. The Ladies' Association held a number of successful events, including luncheons, coffee mornings, and a Jumble sale which was 'not as well attended as usual due to the newspaper strike but which made £180.' Functions enabled the group to donate a clock for the Ladies Gallery in memory of Rabbi Newman. Charitable work also included donating £60 to the local Kosher Meals on Wheels service, £250 to the Association of United Synagogue Ladies Guild towards their project for Waverly Manor House for the Elderly in Hendon.

Other active groups included the Cultural and Literary Society. One evening, Maurice Samuelson, the then London correspondent of the Jewish Telegraphic Agency, gave a talk about his experiences, entitled: 'With Israelis in Cairo.' Of Samuelson's talk, the Annual Report for the synagogue for 1977-8 note of his talk: 'The historic occasion event was the visit of the Israeli delegation to Cairo following the Sadat visit to Jerusalem. Samuelson described the consultations, the emotional reception with the Jews of Cairo on the shul, and the fascinating behaviour of the Cairo Moslems.'

An innovative project was undertaken by the synagogue to host a group of paraplegics from Israel. This was under the auspices of the Golders Green group of the

British Friends of War Disabled. The group with their helpers were welcomed at the synagogue by Dayan Swift and the Defence Attaché, Mrs Nilly Sivron. Special trips for the group included the Houses of Parliament (accompanied by Baroness Serota), Windsor Castle, Brent Cross, Tower of London, Arsenal Football Club, the West End and theatres.

In the autumn of 1977, the synagogue became a Regional Youth Centre where young people could take up studies in spoken Hebrew, O level Hebrew, Jewish History, Drama, cookery, discussion, and Israel Projects. Other such centres were established at synagogues in Hendon, Finchley, Hampstead Garden Suburb and Muswell Hill, with occasional joining of the groups for special meetings.

Mourning the Death of Rabbi Newman

The New Year 1977 was marked by the sudden death of Rabbi Newman who passed away at his home suddenly as he was preparing to go to shul. He had been present for the *Mincha* service in the synagogue the previous evening, but had not arrived the next morning. Dr. Laitner rushed to the house but Rabbi Newman had already passed away. Dayan Swift, Alfred Woolf and Mr. Rubin were informed

Above: View of the bimah dedicated to the memory of Rabbi Newman and designed by his son Winston.

Right: Leslie Green (left) and Dayan Swift, first night Chanukah. COURTESY TERRY SOPEL

immediately, but it was only towards the end of the service that the congregation was informed. The funeral was held the following day and it was noted in the community's records: 'The body was brought into the synagogue prior to the burial, and Hespedin were delivered by Dayan Swift in the synagogue and at the cemetery by the Emeritus Chief Rabbi, Sir Israel Brodie.'

An emergency meeting of the Board of Management was convened at 8.30 p.m. on Thursday 6 January, at which: 'The meeting stood in memory of the late Rabbi Eugene Newman.' The Minute Book notes that: 'Mr Green paid tribute to the memory of their beloved Rabbi who had served the congregation faithfully as spiritual leader for 23 years, and his loss would be felt not only be members of the congregation to whom he was friend and teacher, but by the many institutions with which he was connected in Anglo-Jewry.'

Dayan Swift offered to act as temporary minister and the search began for a new full time minister. The Board of Management turned its attention to the ongoing

discussions over the central bimah and, and a meeting on 18 August 1977, Leslie Green suggested that 'a most suitable memorial to their late Rabbi, and one which he had very much at heart, would be the installation in the synagogue of a central bimah.' Dayan Swift agreed with Leslie Green and added his weight to the idea by stressing the importance of having a central bimah, which was a traditional feature in all orthodox synagogues. After a full discussion, the Board agreed that it would be a fitting memorial to their late Rabbi, and so it was that Rabbi

Newman's son and architect, Winston Newman, was asked to draw up the plans.[142]

Numbers for the religion school continued to decline, such that by now, it had so few pupils that the classrooms of the shul were offered to Pardes House School for use as a nursery. A drop in membership of the shul itself mirrored this, too, although with a total membership standing at 981, the decline was not too drastic.[143] The secretary in his

Charles and Leila Feinmesser.

From left to right: Gabriel White, Nathan Rubin, Mrs Ward, Leslie Green, Harry Ward.

annual report explained this by the deaths of so many members that year. Another drive was undertaken to encourage new members to the shul, but this against the backdrop of an area that had many other shuls to choose from. Children's services continued, nevertheless, and during 1978, these were taken on the basis of a rota by David Crossley, Barry Shaw, Mr D. Oberman, Dr M. Bennett and David Weitz. There was no shortage, however, of outside groups to rent the premises, from the Kosher Cookery Class to a Betar Group. For a period over the summer of 1977, the Lebetkin Hall was given over to B'nei Akiva for Shabbat and High Holy Day services.

Appointment of Rabbi Jonathan Sacks

At a meeting in the Harris Lebekin Hall on 10 August 1978, it was agreed to appoint Rabbi Dr Jonathan Sacks as the new minister of the synagogue. He took up post on 1 September 1978, and the following day, performed his first duty as the new rabbi by giving an address at the consecration of the new central bimah, dedicated to the late Rabbi Newman. Dayan Swift also officiated at the consecration, and the Haftorah was read by Winston Newman. Rabbi Sacks' induction took place in the synagogue on Thursday 14 September. A reception was held afterwards in the Joseph Freedman Hall. For Dayan Swift, in appreciation of his acting as minister for a year, the congregation presented him with a colour television set.

Rabbi Sacks brought to the congregation a vision that centred around new adult education programmes, something which was rare in the 1970s, and also the encouragement of hospitality activities. He suggested that members of the Board might give a Kiddush or Shabbat lunch for visitors and elderly members of the congregation; something which 'members had responded to well.' The adult education programmes attracted people from outside the shul. There was a group for young members, too. The Adult Education Programme was instigated following a meeting in July 1979. A programme was worked out, and, that same year from 16 October, there were three 8-week terms mapped out with lectures on Tuesday evenings, held in the two halls. The lecturers were Rabbi Sacks, David Greenberg, Alan Cohen, and Dr Irving Jacobs. The subjects included Basic Judaism Course, Hebrew Reading for Beginners, and Lectures on the Siddor. The courses were free to members of the synagogue, and £10 per term to non-members.

On 4 March 1979, at a special service in the synagogue, Rabbi Sacks and Rev. Dr. Isaac Levy consecrated the new standard of the Golders Green Association of Jewish Ex-Servicemen and Women. The Cultural and Literary Society resumed activities, and later

---

[142] Winston Newman still has all his original architectural plans for the central bimah.
[143] Membership now stood at 707 males and 274 females.

Induction of Rabbi Jonathan Sacks, 14 September 1978.

that month the guests of honour were the Chief Rabbi and Israeli ambassador. In June, a communal luncheon on Shabbat saw an attendance of 154 people; the catering was arranged by the Ladies' Committee.

With sadness, the congregation mourned the loss of Rev. Livingstone after his death in September 1979 at the age of 94. A memorial service was held in the synagogue, after which Mrs Livingstone thanked 'all concerned for making the memorial service for her late husband such a dignified and memorable occasion.'[144] A Memorial Fund raised £2,000 and was presented to his widow by cheque. In June 1980, the first discussions took place about placing a suitable memorial in the vestibule 'to the memory of the Six Million Martyrs of the Holocaust.'

Thanks were offered to Mrs Lucy White for planting flowers in the borders at the front of the synagogue, totally transforming the area into something which many members appreciated.[145] This she continued to do for many years to come and is mentioned for this work in the Minute Books on a number of occasions. In celebration of the diamond wedding of Dr. and Mrs Strauss, their son in America donated five hundred dollars to the shul. During the early 1980s, many discussions took place in Board meetings about the financial deficit in the annual income of the shul. Security was of concern such that from 1981, an attendant and guard dog were on duty outside the synagogue every Shabbat.

Another brainchild of Rabbi Sacks was the establishment of the Golders Green Group, affectionately known as *The Three Gs*. The group was for people aged

UNITED SYNAGOGUE—ק"ק כנסת ישראל

Golders Green Synagogue
Dunstan Road, N.W.11

The Honorary Officers and Board of Management
request the pleasure of your company

on Thursday, September 14th, 1978—Ellul 12th, 5738, at 7.30 p.m.

on the occasion of the

Induction into Office of Rabbi Jonathan Sacks, M.A. (Cantab.)
as Minister of the Congregation

by The Chief Rabbi, Dr. Immanuel Jakobovits

The Service will be conducted by The Rev. C. Abramovitz
assisted by the Choir under the direction of Mr. Alan Mays

Worshippers are kindly requested   R.S.V.P.   Refreshments after the Service
to be seated by 7.15 p.m.   in the Joseph Freedman Hall

Rev. and Mrs Livingstone on their Diamond Wedding anniversary, 1972.

---

[144] Entry in the Minutes, September 1979.
[145] Minute Book entry, 20 October 1980.

Yakar, study weekend retreats,
Wood Lane, Stanmore.

between 25–40, and consisted of lectures and dinners, chaired for ten years by Brian Beckman. The club provided a social meeting point with lectures, quiz suppers, outings, and dinners; the latter often attended by over sixty people. The monthly three-course dinners were cooked in the shul kitchen by members of the club. Surviving papers from *The Three Gs* reveal the broad range of lectures and topics covered by the group.[146] Speakers addressed the group on such wide ranging topics as: *Community Politics* (Monroe Palmer),[147] *State-Sponsored Terrorism and the PLO Now* (Jillian Becker),[148] *Aspects of the Hagadah* (Rabbi Sacks), *Drinking and Drug Abuse* (Dr Max Glatt),[149] *Torah and Science* (Dr Cyril Domb),[150] *Israel and the Media* (Caroline Thompson),[151] *Current Issues in Social Welfare and Community Care* (Dr John Carter),[152] and *the Disappearing Diplomat* (Maurice Samuelson).[153]

Rabbi Sacks instigated weekends away in a large house in Stanmore from Friday to Sunday, which produced a real bond between members. A new group was formed for children aged 8–13, to meet at the synagogue on Shabbat afternoons. Brian Beckman recalls: 'Rabbi Sacks introduced ceremonies that we had never had before, and started a Sunday morning breakfast for bar mitzvah boys to continue their learning. He was a great speaker and scholar who inspired people. He motivated a lot of good work in the community and encouraged hospitality.'

Myer Harris.

---

[146] Brian Beckman holds many of the papers relating to *The Three Gs* and kindly made these available to the author during the writing of this book.

[147] Member of the congregation and member of the National Liberal Party and local Liberal Candidate. He went on to become a Life Peer.

[148] World renowned expert on terrorism.

[149] Dr Max Glatt was consultant psychiatrist and world authority on alcoholism and drug dependence.

[150] Professor of Theoretical Physics at King's College London.

[151] Commissioning Editor, Channel 4 Television.

[152] Department of Social Science at the London School of Economics.

[153] On the fate of Raoul Wallenberg.

CHAPTER 9

Challenging Times

Golders Green Road, 1980s. COURTESY: HENDON LIBRARY & ARCHIVES

AS THE COMMUNITY at Golders Green Synagogue moved into the 1980s and 90s, communal life remained active even though attendance at services was falling. Upkeep of the large synagogue building and the two halls would prove to be a challenge in the coming decades. The Joseph Freedman Hall was now in dire need of electrical re-wiring. Board member Monroe Palmer proposed 'a levy of £3.00 per male member be made on the Rosh Hashanah account to pay towards the cost of current urgent electrical work.' His motion was seconded by David Clayton, and carried by the rest of the Board. A number of ladies could not make the stairs up to the ladies' gallery due to disability or lack of mobility and it was decided that they ladies could be accommodated for services at the back of the synagogue.[154] The Board noted the congregation was 'indebted to Mrs Lucy White for her devoted work in

beautifying the synagogue grounds by planting flowers.'[155]

The year 1981 saw the honour of a Knighthood bestowed on Chief Rabbi Jakobovits and a letter of congratulations was sent to him on behalf of the synagogue. Rabbi Sacks made an appeal for help with welfare work and this had engendered a good response. During this period, his wife Elaine and Monroe Palmer were joint chairmen of the Welfare Committee for visiting the sick and those in hospital. After the High Holy Days that autumn, chairman Leslie Green, formally offered the Board's thanks to Rabbi Sacks and Rev. Abramovitz 'for the excellent manner in which they conducted the services.' Grateful thanks were also expressed to Dayan Swift for preaching at services in the synagogue and the Joseph Freedman Hall, and to Mr R. Horowitz and Mr M. Horowitz who conducted the overflow services in the Joseph Freedman Hall. The new

[154] Meeting of the Board of Management, 18 May 1981.
[155] Entry in the Minutes, 24 August 1981.

Golders Green Road, 1980s. Golders Green Road, 1980s. COURTESY: HENDON LIBRARY & ARCHIVES

year of 1982 saw another congregant and member of the Board, Monroe Palmer, honoured with an OBE in the New Year's Honour List.

Rev. Abramovitz resigned his position as Reader from 1 May 1982 to take up a similar position at St John's Wood Synagogue. Applicants for his post were invited to visit the shul and participate in a service. Amongst those who wished to be considered for the post were Rev. B Segal and Rev. Joel Portnoy. This same year, Rabbi Sacks resigned his position as minister to take up a post at Jews' College, with effect from 1 June 1982. The Board of Management suggested that new guidelines should be drawn up for the appointment of a new Rabbi. The United Synagogue house which was occupied by Rev. Abramovitz would be reserved for the new minister. The Board and Honorary officers agreed that the seat of the late Rev. Livingstone in the

synagogue was now to be reserved for Rabbi Sacks. Dayan Swift again agreed to act as temporary minister; his second time of serving the community during an interregnum. Rev. Michael Binstock agreed to officiate, too, on Shabbat and High Holy Days. It was decided that the highly successful Adult Education Centre instigated by Rabbi Sacks should continue as a permanent part of the synagogue's life. The new Rabbi would be asked to continue running this alongside Michael Posen, Brian Beckman, David Crossley and Ben Rose.

Financial representative, David Crossley, advised that the synagogue should continue to engage a security guard and dog on Shabbat and Festival mornings. At a special Shabbat service in June 1982, Rev. Leslie Hardman gave the sermon to coincide with the visit to the shul of disabled Israeli ex-servicemen. Later that same month, the minutes

Rabbi Jonathan Sacks, 1980.

Dayan Swift and Terry Sopel.

note 'decorum on Sabbath morning services were deteriorating.'[156]

The synagogue participated in meetings of the local Hendon and Golders Green Branch of the Council of Christians and Jews. The shul's representative on it for sometime was Monroe Palmer. His wife, Susette, was chairman of the synagogue's Hebrew classes for a number of years. In 1982, Miss Goldberg retired as headteacher 'as

she was getting married.' The Parents/Teacher Association was revived, with new chairman Alan Cowan. Numbers for religion school stood at between thirty-five and forty attending on Sundays, and eighteen to twenty on Tuesdays. The Classes Committee (1983) consisted of Leslie Green, Mr L. Kleerekoper, Monroe Palmer, Co-opted: Brian Beckman, Mr M. Cohen, Mr A. Cohen, Mr H. Goldblum, Mrs Susette Palmer, Mrs R. Martin-Sklan, and Mr B. Shannon. Serving on the Choir and Services Committee at this time were Ralph Cohen, Dr L. D. Jacobs, Mr. Lionel Land, Mr M. Land, Alan Mays, Michael Mays and Dr S. Torrance.

Rabbi Dayan Ivan Binstock

Ivan Binstock, who was to finish *Semicha* in Israel in September 1983, expressed an interest in becoming the new Rabbi at Golders Green. At a meeting on 26 August 1982, the following resolution was passed: 'The Board of Management invites Rev. Ivan Binstock to become minister/preacher of the Golders Green Synagogue from 1 September 1983.'

In the meantime, the High Holy Day services for 1982 were successful. Chief Rabbi Immanuel Jakobovits attended the services on Kol Nidrei and Yom Kippur which was a great honour for the community. Rev. Michael Binstock continued on a temporary basis as the Reader. High Holy Day Services for 1982 were very successful due to Dayan Swift, Rev. Binstock, Rabbi Dr Sacks, Alan Mays and the Choir, Brian Beckman and Mr. L. Kleerekoper. At the end of the year, the appointment of Rev. Ivan Binstock as the new Rabbi for the following September was ratified by the Placement Committee of the United Synagogue.[157] At a meeting on 26 June 1983, the Board formally agreed to appoint him as the new minister from 1 September 1983.

The synagogue, now almost sixty-five years old, and other buildings were in urgent need of maintenance and repair. The fabric and roof of the synagogue, in particular, began to show signs of structural deterioration. It is a huge building to maintain and inevitably, raising the finances for such a potentially expensive renovation programme was of deep concern. The situation of the building and safety would become urgent within two years. Leslie Green stressed the difficulties facing the Functions and Fund-raising Committee.[158] It was suggested that a major fund-raising event should take place in the form of an inaugural dinner for Rev. Binstock on the fourth night of Chanukah. A special printed brochure with advertisements was printed to raise extra funds. The interior of the Lebetkin Hall required renovations at a cost of £450. Re-wiring and electrical work on the classrooms was already underway. There were discussions, too, about the installation of a new

---

[156] Entry in the Minutes, 17 June 1982.
[157] Entry in the Minutes of the Golders Green Synagogue, 6 December 1982.
[158] Discussed at a meeting of the Board on 4 July 1983.

boiler for the synagogue, to change from oil to gas, estimated at £10,630.

The autumn of 1983 was the first year since its early foundations that the synagogue did not hold overflow services for the High Holy Days. Then came the news of the passing of Dayan Swift and Morris Rose. The Minutes note: 'The Chairman paid a warm tribute to the memory of the late Dayan Swift and said that his passing was a great loss to the Golders Green community and the Anglo-Jewish community. He also paid tribute to the late Morris Rose, a highly respected and active member of the Board of Management for many years.'[159] A memorial service and unveiling of a plaque for Dayan Swift took place the following year.[160]

On 24 October, Rabbi Binstock was welcomed to his first meeting of the Board since taking up office. He outlined his intention to revive the Hebrew and religion classes and continue the adult education lectures. Michael Mays asked about the pictures that had been found in the synagogue attic, and the Chairman replied that these had been auctioned at Sotheby's and they had received the last cheque for the final sale. The total amount realised was £600 for the Synagogue Amenities Fund. At this time, Rev. Michael Binstock, who had been acting part-time on a week-to-week basis, was formally appointed part time

Reader on a salary of £4,500 per annum, including High Holy Days and shivas. It was decided to move Friday evening services to the Lebetkin Hall, rather than the main synagogue for a trial period of six months.

Long-standing devoted member Harry Ward retired from the Board, with thanks offered to him for 32 years of devoted service. He founded the Israel Zangwill Foundation, becoming heavily involved in it as an expert in the man's works. He collected an impressive library which has been bequeathed to the Parkes Library at Southampton University as the HS Ward Collection. An active member of the Jewish Historical Society, he became a learned amateur book collector, too. A farewell cocktail party was held in the synagogue in his honour the Sunday following his retirement from the Board.

Community Life

The passing of two stalwarts of the congregation was mourned in February 1984 with the deaths of Alfred Woolf, OBE and Lionel Land. Mrs Paula Goldblum had taken charge of the Hebrew Classes on a voluntary basis. The classes continued to receive funds from the Board of Education, with any shortfall made up from synagogue's own funds. Although the congregation was not experiencing growth, it was still a welcoming and warm community. It was noted that: 'Mr. H. Knobil stated that in his past thirty years' experience of various United Synagogues, he had not come across a more welcoming congregation then Golders Green Synagogue.'[161]

Behaviour during services was a call for concern yet again, with the Minutes making reference to decorum on Simchat Torah being such that 'the meaning of the service was lost in a melee of noise and throwing of sweets and that this year things had gone too far and that the services had

Daniel Rose receives Sir Isaac & Lady Edith Wolfson prize from Mrs Brodie, 7 June 1964.

---

[159] Entry dated 24 October 1983.
[160] Unveiling took place on 8 September 1985.
[161] Entry in the Minutes, 14 May 1984.

completely disintegrated.'[162] A long discussion ensued about what could be done to restore a sense of propriety, especially with regard to the practice of throwing sweets from the Ladies' gallery which had 'become a dangerous habit.' The Board decided to forbid the practice of throwing sweets from the gallery thereafter.

Amongst the gifts donated to the synagogue were a portable ark to hold a Sefer Torah for shivas, donated by Leslie Green, and a large cooker for the kitchen, given by Monroe Palmer. On 5 March 1985, the Golders Green and Hendon branch of the Council of Christians and Jews held its annual meeting in the Lebetkin Hall, addressed by Executive Director Rev. Marcus Braybrooke. Ben Rose later reported back to the Board: 'although the cause is not popular (ie not well attended), the meetings improved relationships between Christians and Jews.'

In Jewish communities across Britain, concern was mounting for Soviet Jewry under the oppressive, often brutal, Cold War regime. Leslie Green was appointed the Golders Green representative at the United Synagogue Committee for Soviet Jewry and attended meetings.

In 1985, Hebrew classes totalled some 47 children. Classes started with a breakfast Minyan led by Rabbi Binstock. Mrs Margolin was now the headteacher, with four other teachers taking classes.

Occasionally, local synagogues in north-west London held joint events to mark moments of national significance. So, on 8 May 1985, the 40th anniversary of VE Day was marked by a Service of Thanksgiving at Hendon Synagogue,

Marriage of Paul Lang and Verna Shisler, 7 March 1989.

attended by members of the Golders Green Synagogue. Around this time, Rabbi Binstock suggested that the shul should have its own magazine, an idea that was well received. He was nominated editor-in-chief, aided by Maurice Samuelson as editor and David Crossley as advertising manager. The magazine became a regular feature and included articles submitted by members. Membership of the shul in 1985 stood at 580 males and 266 females, a total membership of 846. Overflow services resumed for the High Holy Days. Towards the end of the festivals, the Ladies' Guild gave a very successful reception after Succot.

Pideon Ha'ben of Joel Sopel, officiated by Rabbi Binstock, 2 Sept 1985.

---

[162] Board of Management meeting, 30 July 1984.

Lucy White at the synagogue, 1980s.

The synagogue gardens tended by Lucy White.

The state of the building continued to be of concern. In August 1985, it was reported that urgent repairs were needed. The coping on the roof was in a dangerous position, and the roof leaking. Basic costs of repairs inside and outside the shul were estimated at £50,000. A serious defect in the pipes from the Joseph Freedman Hall to the boiler required estimated repairs of £1,500.

During 1986, the adult education programme was thriving. The shul magazine had become extremely popular, edited now solely by Maurice Samuelson, and the advertising section run by David Crossley who had also undertaken duties as Honorary Shammas. Members of the youth took part in the Shabbat morning service occasionally. Mr B. Cowan and Eric Davis acted as Welfare Officers for the shul to visit sick members and those in hospital. Pastoral duties were also undertaken by Kitty Weitz, Molly Greenby and Lucy White.

The women of the shul remained particularly active with their various organisations, and continued to raise funds for various charities. The shul's annual report for 1986 made particular reference to the women who 'carried out their duties in a most conscientious manner.' They had excelled themselves in 'preparing and looking after the Succah, in preparing the Simchas Torah reception and a communal luncheon, and it is hoped that many more ladies will join this devoted band.'

Lucy White continued to tend the synagogue garden as well as organising the flower decorations in the synagogue for Shavuot. A sale of the flowers afterwards raised £100 for synagogue funds. It was noted that a regular Shiur was held just for the ladies, led by Dayan Ehrentreu.

Donations to the synagogue during 1986, included money to establish a brides' room, given by the following members: Mr and Mrs Monroe Palmer on the marriage of their son John to Edith Melinek, Mr and Mrs Tarn on the occasion of the marriage of their son Jeremy, and Mr H. Nagler in memory of his late mother. The carpet for the brides' room was given by Mr H. M. Littner, and the accessories donated by the Ladies' Association.

The 1990s

The community began to experience a sharp decline in membership, with children numbers in the Hebrew classes falling fast due in part to the number of children in the community now attending Jewish primary schools and not needing or wanting to attend on a Sunday morning. A drive was undertaken to encourage new membership for a congregation that now numbered under eight hundred.

On 16 September 1990, a memorial service was held for Rev. Moise Taschlicky. The officiating clergy were Rabbi Ivan Binstock, who gave the memorial address, Rabbi David Katanka, Rev. Michael Binstock, Rev. S. Brickman, Rev. L. Sherman and Rev. M. Taylor; and the choir directed by Emmanuel Fisher.

Internal struggles, with falling synagogue memberships and problems of increasing assimilation, were

Advert, 1986.

Adverts, 1980s.

affecting Anglo-Jewish communities during the 1990s, and Golders Green was no exception. The community, however, continued to look outwards and in particular helped fellow communities that had lived for forty years under Communism.

During the Cold War, life had been increasingly difficult for Jewish communities in Communist countries. Changes in Eastern Europe which would have been unthinkable just a few years before led to an uprising from the grass roots and Communism began to collapse and with it, the old Eastern bloc countries. After the fall of the Berlin Wall in 1989, the United Synagogue encouraged congregations to twin with Jewish communities formerly behind the Iron Curtain. Golders Green Synagogue decided to twin with Zaparozhye in the Ukraine, a small community with a population of 800,000, of which 16,000 were Jews, and a further 4,000 Jews living in neighbouring towns. Not only had it suffered under Communism, but the town was occupied in the Second World War by the Germans. The town has a mass grave of 1,000 Jewish victims of the Holocaust.

In February 1994, two members of Golders Green Synagogue, Mike Posen and David Reuben, visited Zaparozhye. They found an enthusiastic community, but one bereft after living under a repressive Soviet regime. The government eventually handed back the main synagogue that had been confiscated under the Communist regime. In 1995, Golders Green Synagogue helped the community acquire its first Sefer Torah. Help continued in the ensuing years with the congregation raising funds to facilitate Jewish life and education: two Sifrei Torah, a new roof and

kitchen for the nursery, sports equipment and a gymnasium for the children's home, plus funding for the annual Passover Sedarim, which is attended by around 2000 people. It was a positive project that benefitted the revival of Jewish religious life in the former Eastern bloc.

In 1995, Golders Green Synagogue's historic connections to civic life came to the fore again when its member Susette Palmer was elected Mayor of Barnet, the first Liberal mayor ever elected to the borough. Dayan Binstock was appointed the Mayor's chaplain for the year. Susette Palmer's inauguration civic ceremony took place in the synagogue on 1 October, during which a special prayer was recited:

> 'Lord of the Universe, bestow Your blessings upon the Mayor, Councillor Susette Palmer and the Mayor's Escort, Mr Monroe Palmer, during their Mayoral Year. We ask You to bless the Councillors, the officers and staff of the Council and all those who guide the destiny of this Borough.'

The ceremony, officiated by Dayan Binstock and Rabbi Katanka, included a Prayer for the Queen and the Royal Family, Prayer for the Welfare of the State of Israel, music by the choir, led by Alan Mays, and the National Anthem. A Guard of Honour was provided by the Jewish Lads' Brigade.

The following year, the community celebrated another anniversary – eighty years since its foundation. The year focused on looking back over its history, alongside numerous celebrations that included a cantorial concert on 28 January, and an exhibition during the summer

Induction ceremony in the synagogue of Susette Palmer as Mayor of Barnet, 1995.

Susette Palmer, Mayor of Barnet, 1995.

Rabbi David Katanka.

months.[163] The then chairman of the synagogue, Robin Summers, commented: 'We want to look back at our roots. We have extensive documentation and records, and this will be a fascinating and exciting event. Our membership declined because young people were unable to move into the area. Due to lower house prices, they are coming back and the community is once again thriving.'[164]

Dayan Binstock commented at the time of the anniversary: 'The shul can look back on a rich history and has the resources to look forward to an exciting future.' It was already known then that he was going to leave the congregation to take up the post of Rabbi at St John's Wood Synagogue. Through the next period, the synagogue's chazan, David Katanka, who had received *Semicha*, was eventually appointed its Rabbi and led the congregation through one of the most troubled times in its history. During the 1990s, many Jewish communities were struggling with identity and assimilation, falling attendance at services; the tide of which has only turned around in the new millennium due to a renaissance of Jewish life and learning.

Tensions had already begun to emerge between members who followed the more traditional 'United Synagogue style of service' and who wished to keep the status quo and those who wanted to steer the community towards a more informal modern orthodox style of service. This tension led to some extremely difficult times and Golders Green Synagogue entered a rocky period that would take nearly a generation to resolve.

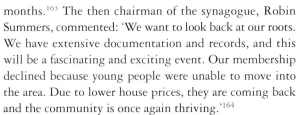

London Borough of Barnet

Councillor SUSETTE PALMER BA(Hons)
MAYOR

ORDER OF

CIVIC SERVICE

AT THE

Golders Green Synagogue
Dunstan Road, London NW11

ON

SUNDAY 1ST OCTOBER 1995
at 11.00 am

Conducted by
DAYAN IVAN BINSTOCK BSc
Mayor's Chaplain
with Rabbi David Katanka MA

M M CALLER BSc(Eng) C Eng
MICE MCIWEM FRSA CDipAF
Chief Executive

---

[163] Announced in the *Jewish Chronicle*, 12 January 1996.
[164] *Jewish Chronicle*, 12 January 1996.

CHAPTER 10
Regeneration and Revival

FROM A MEMBERSHIP of nearly fifteen hundred in its heyday, the Golders Green Synagogue experienced a sharp demographic decline to around five hundred members at this low point. The religion school had effectively ceased to exist and to an outside observer, it looked as if there was a possibility that the community would not survive. Whilst the community genuinely sought to fulfill the needs of all members, the clash between traditional and modern views led to some extremely difficult times and the community faced fracture for nearly a decade.

The main area of contention was whether to preserve the synagogue services in the traditional more formal 'United Synagogue' style led by a Chazan, or make the services less formal and more participatory by encouraging individual members to lead services and the congregation to join in the singing. The difficulty of preserving the traditional approach was that the membership was in sharp

decline and in particular, the younger generation no longer wished to participate in the traditional formal services and were looking to go elsewhere. Some members could foresee that if it continued on this path, the synagogue would be forced to close as it became a financially and logistically unviable congregation. The members who wanted to introduce a modern orthodox service, with more community participation, saw their approach as a way of attracting younger members and thereby revitalising the congregation. Tensions rose as the issues were hotly debated time and again at Board meetings.

Eventually, an agreement was reached between the two sides that once or twice a month, the Friday night service could take place in the more informal setting of the Joseph Freedman Hall, and a separate Shabbat morning service would be held in the Lebetkin Hall. 'The trial proved so successful,' comments Peter Zinkin, 'that the Honorary

The New Minyan, Joseph Freedman Hall. COURTESY SARAH KENDAL

Joe Friedman.

Officers took fright and the decision to allow the Shabbat service in the Lebetkin Hall was rescinded.' This led to the alternative minyan, or 'New Minyan', taking the decision to move out of the shul to the nearby Jewish Vegetarian Society in Finchley Road, with services arranged by Benny Chain, Brian Beckman, Stephen Shaw and Adam Winton. Benny Chain recalls: 'The first New Minyan service took place just before Rosh Hashanah (Jewish New Year). All the young people came to the services and we were not expecting quite such numbers. The atmosphere was fantastic. The service was full and we had over a hundred people.' Thereafter, the services attracted an average of sixty people on a regular weekly basis. Members of the New Minyan retained their membership of Golders Green Synagogue, and after some months the New Minyan decided to make a concerted drive to be elected to the Board of Management of the main synagogue. An election took place in which Alan Mays, Brian Beckman and Peter Zinkin stood for the Board. There was a huge turn-out and the existing Honorary Officers were re-elected; however, the fact that there was a challenge was the start of a process that would eventually lead to major change within the community.

The election almost triggered a split within the Golders Green Synagogue because, following the vote, the New Minyan seriously considered the idea of establishing its own separate shul. 'A fracture would have had devastating consequences for the future of the community,' says Peter Zinkin, 'It could have resulted in two separate non-viable shuls. We consulted the President of the United Synagogue, Elkan Levy, and he suggested that we hold a referendum to ask the congregation if they preferred a split or for the New Minyan to come back to the shul and hold its own separate services in the hall. The overwhelming majority voted in favour of the hall.'

Within a short space of time, some of the longstanding members of the Board had served their six-year maximum term of office and could not stand for re-election. Peter Zinkin and Joe Friedman then stood for office and were elected unopposed to the Board. This was the stepping stone to a new future. Peter Zinkin was chairman of the shul, with Jackie Crossley as vice-chair, and Joe Friedman as warden of the Old Minyan and then Benny Chain as warden and chair of the New Minyan.[165] Benny Chain, Joe Friedman and Peter Zinkin persuaded the New Minyan to move back to the main premises, and hold its services in the Joseph Freedman Hall. For almost a decade, the synagogue functioned as two separate minyanim for Shabbat services; one with the more formal traditional service that worshipped in the main synagogue, the other reflecting the more modern orthodox approach of the services in the Jewish Vegetarian Society. Both minyanim came together for the daily services, Kiddush after the Shabbat service, and combined youth services for the small number of young members of the congregation. The idea was to try to operate as one community wherever possible. The appointment of Rabbi Belovski came at a fortuitous time as the two minyanim were beginning to learn to live together and he helped bridge the gap between them. In addition, all social events were for everyone.

The move to two separate services had coincided with a realisation that the nature of the community was already changing. The Old Minyan began to decline because of natural attrition, and some of its people moving away. Peter Zinkin reflects on this difficult period: 'There was a perception in the Old Minyan that people in the New Minyan were elitist. I believe this was largely unfounded, but it caused a number of tensions and took a decade for the angst to settle down. The key player who sparked the road to a new community was Benny Chain – the visionary, the revolutionary – who was elected chairman in 2009. Along with others who helped to implement the vision, the redevelopment of the community became a highly motivated successful team effort and led to one of the most ambitious projects since the community was founded in 1915.'

Major Redevelopment

One of the challenges faced by the community was the outside perception that it was an antiquated congregation that was old-fashioned, rigidly orthodox and over traditional. But this belied the reality of a congregation that was religiously tolerant with a unique and inclusive philosophy. The new members of the Board decided to try to raise the substantial sums of money needed for the repairs to the synagogue. They were aware that enormous sums were needed – initial estimates were in the region of three million pounds. A successful application to English Heritage secured a grant of £100,000 for repairs to the synagogue roof.

---

[165] He held the position of warden until 2005.

Synagogue interior in dire need of urgent repairs. COURTESY PETER ZINKIN

The successful application to English Heritage sparked a move to look at the general future of the congregation and find ways to regenerate its membership. At a meeting in January 2011, the Board voted overwhelmingly to support a 'vigorous rebranding and marketing strategy to portray Golders Green as the inclusive, friendly and committed community it really is.'[166] Benny Chain and his daughter Rachel Clark suggested an ambitious project – to build a Jewish state primary school behind the synagogue premises, an idea which coincided with the government's new initiative to support the establishment of 'free schools' and provide grants for such schools. This suggestion was to lead to the critical turning point in the community's recent history.

Part of the rebranding was to deal with the abysmal condition of the community buildings, including renovation of the synagogue itself. No one underestimated the challenge at a time when the average age of the membership was over the age of 60, and numbers were continuing to fall. 'The challenges were enormous,' comments Rabbi Belovski. 'When we started, the Grade II listed synagogue suffered from severe physical dilapidation.'

The roof needed replacing, it not being watertight, which caused further damage to the fabric of the building. The exterior brickwork was damaged in several places and needed replacing. The interior décor was completely ruined. The infrastructure, heating electrics and plumbing were outdated, and the interior was generally cold and damp. A report read:

> 'The many auxiliary rooms are in a state of disrepair, and many are dangerous and not fit for purpose... The redevelopment must somehow provide an intimacy and warmth which invites and encourages participation, by both men and women, in a communal spiritual experience.'[167]

Alongside the major renovations, a plan was put together to move the new minyan from the Joseph Freedman Hall back into the main synagogue. It included bringing the women downstairs from the Ladies' Gallery during services and having a *mehitzah* (screen) to separate the men's section from the women's, and developing the interior of the shul in such a way that it can be used as a function space when not in use for services. Because the synagogue was Grade II listed, any changes to the interior also had to be approved by English Heritage and Barnet Council. Permission for the changes was secured.

Further funds were raised: a grant of £100,000 from the Maurice and Vivienne Wohl Foundation for the

Rear of the synagogue after demolition of the Joseph Freedman Hall & Lebetkin Hall, 2013. COURTESY MAURICE SAMUELSON

---

[166] Document/report: *Past, Present and Future: The Regeneration of the Golders Green United Synagogue Community.*
[167] *Past, Present and Future: The Regeneration of the Golders Green United Synagogue Community.*

Interior of Refurbished shul.

Beth Hamedrash for daily services.

refurbishment of the building and also £25,000 from the DCMS National Churches Trust for renovation of the synagogue kitchens. Remarkably, over a million pounds was raised from within the congregation itself.

The success of the fund raising programme led to a major refurbishment of the synagogue, part of which involved the removal of pews at the back of the prayer hall to accommodate a Beth Hamidrash for the daily *Minyan*, and a leveling of the floor to provide a new space for community and social functions.

A reconfiguration of the seating in the front of the main synagogue provided a better space for prayer for both men and women. Some of the redevelopment work replaced facilities lost by the demolition of the two halls: a new kitchen, toilets, bride's room, Board room and office. Refurbishment also included the commissioning of a new Ner Tamid (eternal flame) and two new Parochets (curtains covering the Ark) by American Judaica artist Michael Gore. Michael, who works between Venice and America, also created a new set of covers to match the Parochets, and a smaller Ner Tamid for Rimon. He commented on the Ner Tamid:

'I envisioned an elegant, graceful shape in Venetian glass that would complement the *bimah* both in colour and scale, bringing a refined, elegant counterpoint to the Parochets and *bimah* in general. I blew into the glass hundreds of spiralling bubbles, representing my concept of L'Dor Va'Dor. The bubbles in the *Ner Tamid* change in size and shape as they rise throughout the glass and represent the past and future generations of our people.'[168]

The community had its own design guru in Brian Baderman who created the design for the new *bimah* and *mehitzah*, and arranged the manufacture of both. The dedication of the new *bimah* and reading desk took place on 7 September 2014. The Ark was refurbished in memory of Leslie Green, a former chairman and warden of the synagogue. The Board Room was given a make-over, furnished with wooden boards and skylights, becoming a popular venue for weekday services and shiurim (Torah lessons). Here the weekly toddler service takes place, with over thirty toddlers. In December 2013, the new Beth Hamidrash was created with a library, and the Brides Room refurbished. Benny Chain comments: 'To attract young people, we needed to move back into a refurbished shul. Having raised the money, this was possible. Rabbi Belovski was supportive of both minyanim, and he helped to bring the community back together.'

The new bimah.

---

[168] The GGS Journal, September 2013.

The new Jewish Primary School.

Rimon Jewish Primary School

At the centre of the regeneration programme was the building of a new Jewish primary school which would encourage membership of young families and the next generation, to ensure survival and growth. The Jewish day school was first approved by the Department of Education for pre-opening in October 2011. The idea was first conceived ten months earlier in January 2011 as the brainchild of Benny Chain and Rachel Clark. Together they worked on a grant application in record time, with very little hope that it would be successful. However, the project was one of the 42 projects out of over 1500 to be accepted for funding. Rachel Clark later became the school's first chair of governors.

The vision depended on a successful application to the Department of Education for government funding, but the route to securing that funding was not guaranteed and required much work by the steering committee which consisted of Rachel Clark, Benny and Julia Chain, and David and Samantha Vaughan. This group, with the great help of Peter Zinkin, worked tirelessly in negotiations with the Department of Education and the United Synagogue to make the community's vision a reality and spur the revival project. 'Initially the United Synagogue, which saw only a dying congregation, doubted the regeneration programme and questioned the need for another Jewish school,' says Julia Chain, 'Benny had many long and difficult meetings with sceptical officers of the United

One of the classrooms, Rimon Jewish Primary School.

Synagogue, but finally persuaded them of the congregation's vitality and strong motivation to revive the synagogue. When the school eventually opened, there was much enthusiasm within the United Synagogue.'

Making way for the new school building involved the demolition of three old buildings at the rear of the synagogue: the large classroom block which once housed the caretaker's flat, the Lebetkin Hall which contained the succah and Beth Hamidrash, and the Joseph Freedman Hall. These brick buildings had played a central role in the early community, but now it was time to make way for the future.

In September 2012, the Rimon Jewish Primary School opened its doors to its first pupils. A new free school, the first of its kind as a Jewish community school in Golders Green, appointed Dr Zoe Dunn as its founding

Lord Sacks and Rabbi Belovski, the opening of the Rimon Jewish Primary School, 2012.

headteacher. She had been raised and educated in Kent and was a graduate of Homerton College, Cambridge. Commenting on her appointment, she said that she was interested in: 'the diverse and varied culture of Golders Green and so being appointed as a non-Jewish head of a Jewish school is a challenge that appeals to me.'[169]

The school has proved a huge success. Receiving its inaugural Ofsted inspection during 2014, the inspectors agreed that what had been achieved was 'nothing short of a miracle.'[170] Rabbi Belovski comments:

'The school is now full and oversubscribed with a waiting list. It has breathed new life into our congregation because families are coming to synagogue services. We have over 70 children at youth services. So successful is the Shabbat morning toddlers' service that we have a delightful Shabbat morning problem – where to safely store all the baby buggies. This remarkable achievement has meant that the congregation has just appointed a young modern Orthodox Rabbinic couple, Rabbi Sam Fromson and Hadassah Fromson, to help with the expanding youth work. The current challenge is for the new younger generation to take on

leadership roles within the community and on the Board to ensure the continued success of the revival. And I feel energized by these changes, almost as if I am serving a new shul.'

The school is now under the leadership of the current Governors, led by its outstanding chairperson, David Vaughan.

Lord Sacks and children of the community at the opening of Rimon Jewish Primary School.

[169] The GGS Journal, September 2012.
[170] The GGS Journal, April 2014.

Community Life

The drive towards growth of community membership has also given rise to a variety of proactive groups. These have included: "Dress" (now renamed GGE, Golders Green Events) – a social club for all ages that runs events ranging from ice-skating to guided walks and theatre; also "Chevra" – a social dynamic for aged 20-40s to reach out to those who are unaffiliated to any synagogue; and a special social-based programme for the over 70s. The jewel in the crown is a full programme for children aged 2-17. In particular, the children's services, designed and managed for many years by Dr Jo Hochauser, have been an enormous success and have been key in bringing back young families to the community. Jo designed a system where older children are trained to run services for the younger ones, and these have been successful, not only in their own terms, but also in developing leadership skills among the youth of the congregation. "Graduates" of Dunstan Road youth also play a key role in B'nei Akiva and other communal activities. The sense of a cohesive congregation is reflected in articles and news items which appear in a biannual colour shul magazine, edited by Joel Clark.

Congregant Penina Bowman has been involved in gaining approval for the Eruv to be extended to cross over the Hendon Way, thus helping a number of members to come to services who otherwise would find it difficult on Shabbat. It would also encourage new membership for young families by increasing the range of available housing, enabling the bringing of buggies, and attendance at synagogue.

In 2009, the idea of Mitzvah Day was established, now a major annual fund-raising event for the relief of poverty and hardship, focusing on local and national projects. Liz Manuel and Samantha Vaughan tirelessly run the activities for Golders Green, and Mitzvah Day is now well established in the community calendar. In the Joseph Freedman Hall, Susette Palmer organised a knitathon where members of the congregation knitted squares for two blankets that were donated to World Jewish Relief in memory of Rosalind Beckman. This was alongside a donation of 43 bin bags of unwanted clothes from congregants, also given to World Jewish Relief for distribution in Eastern Europe. Locally, volunteers collected extra tins and items of food outside Sainsburys that generated 12 large crates of food for Cricklewood Homeless Concern. The youth of the congregation also helped on Mitzvah Day by supporting the Chicken Soup Shelter in Stamford Hill, by making sandwiches and volunteering at the shelter.

Purim, 2013.

Purim, 2013.

In 2014, Mitzvah Day again included collecting donations of food for Cricklewood Homeless Concern and knitting for World Jewish Relief. Volunteers collected extra tins and items of food outside Sainsburys that generated 12 large crates of food for Cricklewood Homeless Concern. The youth of the congregation also helped on Mitzvah Day by supporting the Chicken Soup Shelter in Stamford Hill, by making sandwiches and volunteering at the shelter. A group of volunteers cooked a three-course meal in the synagogue kitchen and donated it to feed 12 homeless people and 3 staff at Barnet Night Shelter. The younger members of the community made cards for Jewish soldiers serving in the armed forces, with older children making biscuits for nurses at the Royal Free Hospital. At the back of the synagogue hall, the area was converted into a blood donation centre for the day that enabled 103 units of blood to be taken from members of the Jewish community and friends. The synagogue has now become the local blood donation centre for the district.

Changes within the United Synagogue, especially regarding the role of women in the community, are also enabling a renaissance of Jewish life. On 14 July 2014, history was made when the United Synagogue elected four women as trustees for the first time for six years. One of those women was Jacqui Zinkin, for six years vice-chairman (and acting Chair) of the Golders Green Synagogue. As Jacqui herself commented: 'We are not called women trustees or lady trustees, or even female trustees. We are

simply trustees. There are no longer any caveats, no longer an imbalance in responsibilities. The trustees who happen to be of the female gender are simply trustees.' Jacqui is also working hard towards wider women's issues in the community, including education and women's experiences of being Jewish.

The congregation's long tradition of links to national and local civic life came to the fore once again when in January 2011, Liberal Democrat Councillor and congregant Monroe Palmer was given a Peerage and inducted as a member of the House of Lords. At the beginning of the millennium, longstanding member Jeremy Manuel had been awarded an OBE in the millennium Honours List for services to Gaucher Disease, a rare genetically inherited disorder that is prevalent in, but not exclusive to, Ashkenazi Jews. More recently, Richard Verber was elected as the senior vice-president of the Board of Deputies.

The year 2013 saw the deaths of two stalwarts of the congregation: Joe Friedman and Adrian Jacobs. Joe Friedman and his wife Yaffe had joined the synagogue in the 1970s. Of refugee background, Joe had survived the Nazi occupation of Hungary by being hidden in a safe house. After the war, he founded a leather goods business that became nationally successful. From the 1990s, he entered the property business and became a developer. Living almost opposite the shul was of huge benefit to the congregation, as reflected in an article about his life in the

Mitzvah Day.

Interior of Refurbished shul.

congregation's magazine which said: 'His experience in property enabled him to attend to the fabric of the shul building: he thought nothing of clambering onto the roof to investigate some problem. On one occasion he physically tackled a suspicious visitor on the bimah. On another, he averted disaster by putting out a fire caused by a defective electrical circuit.'[171] In the congregation's hundred-year history, Joe Friedman and Brian Beckman are the only two congregants to be honoured with a special designation

'chaver' – only given to very special people in the congregation.

Joe Friedman threw himself into the life of the community, and his level-headed advice on communal matters was respected. He did an enormous amount of good work for the community which he loved. On his death in May 2013, over two hundred people gathered at the shul to pay their respects before his body was flown to Israel for burial.

---

[171] The GGS Journal, September 2013.

Adrian Jacobs, former financial representative of the shul, also passed away in 2013. He had grown up in the East End and later settled in Golders Green. Later, he agreed to become the financial representative at a time when the congregation was experiencing much transition and change. He happily carried out the unenviable task of chasing up lapsed membership fees and thereby improved the finances of the shul. When he stepped down in this role, the community conferred on him the honour of *Chatan Torah*.

Centenary Celebrations

For the Centenary of the foundation of the community in 2015, a number of special events were organised under the

chairmanship of Julia Chain. The first of these was the Centenary Sabbath Service on Saturday 20 June in the presence of the Chief Rabbi, Ephraim Mirvis, attended by the Mayor and Mayoress, local dignitaries, MP and Christian leaders.

In his address, Chief Rabbi Mirvis spoke about continuity linking back to the patriarch Isaac, a continuity that adapted to new circumstances and enabled the revival that marks the congregation as unique in the United Synagogue today. In his sermon, Rabbi Dr Belovski underlined the successful partnership of rabbinic and lay leadership which has underpinned the growth of the congregation to enable it to enter its second century with confidence and a future. A special Centenary Prayer was written for the occasion:

Purim, 2014.

Refurbished interior, showing a new versatile space at the back of the shul.

May He who blessed our ancestors Abraham, Isaac and Jacob, bless this holy congregation - Kehillat Kennesset Yisrael Golders Green - as it completes 100 years from the year of its founding. May He also bless all those who visit it to pray, all its leaders from the day of its inception until now, all its supporters and all those who are occupied with its needs. May the merit of its founders and their aspirations stand for us today and for the generations that will follow us. May the Holy One, may He be blessed, send blessing and success upon all the works of our hands and may He grant length of days to this holy congregation with peace and insight until the coming of the redeemer. Let us say: Amen.

The service was followed by a celebratory Kiddush, held in an area of the synagogue that can be adapted for such events. A special exhibition of the community's history was commissioned, written and curated by the author, and displayed in the shul for the first time at the Centenary Shabbat service, where it remained for the duration of 2015.

To The Future

Today, the synagogue has been transformed from a tired, dilapidated building to a modern, regenerated place of prayer. There is still some work to carry out on the building and on the synagogue gardens.[172] The growing congregation looks forward to its future. The aims of the original regeneration programme have been successfully fulfilled, ensuring that the community can 'develop, grow and retain its place as a driving force in Anglo-Jewry.'

The community seeks to pool its resources and skills for the benefit of the religious life of the synagogue and it has led to a very vibrant congregation that is building for the future. Today, as Benny Chain explains, the congregation aligns itself 'with the objectives at the heart of the United Synagogue's own philosophy. It is no coincidence that despite its relatively small size, its membership roll has boasted not only a Chief Rabbi, but a disproportionate number of leaders of Anglo Jewry who have contributed very substantially to shaping the life of the wider Jewish community.'[173]

---

[172] In 2015, one section of the synagogue gardens was replanted and dedicated to the late Lucy White who had spent so much time tending the flower beds.

[173] Document/report: *Past, Present and Future: The Regeneration of the Golders Green United Synagogue Community*, copy lent to the author.

Bar mitzvah of Gabriel Frank, 2014.

Beth Hamedrash for daily services.

In this new millennium, Golders Green and its neighbouring areas represent one of the most densely populated Jewish localities in the UK. It is home to a range of differing Jewish religious expressions, from ultra-Orthodox to Orthodox to Liberal and Reform. 'It is a congregation filled with academics,' says Rabbi Belovski. 'We maintain the United Synagogue ethos, irrespective of level of observance, whilst not diluting the quality of the religious life. At our core is a serious modern Orthodox Judaism, with a willingness to think deeply and bring in creative speakers. We maintain the broadest appeal whilst not diminishing the message. It has a powerful partnership between Rabbi and lay leadership.'

'There is so much loyalty to the community,' says Julia Chain. 'There are families at the shul today who are fifth or sixth generation members. What the Golders Green Synagogue is experiencing today is a complete renaissance. None of this would have been possible without the very generous donations of many members of the congregation and their families.'

Interior of the synagogue with the bimah and Ark, 2015.

Centenary Exhibition of the Synagogue's history, 2015.

APPENDIX 1
Officers of the Congregation

This appendix gives the main officers of the congregation during its hundred-year history and, for some selective years, also the members who sat on the Board of Management.

1915
President	Benjamin Drage
Vice President	J. Victor
Treasurer	Sol Karet

1916
President	Benjamin Drage
Vice President	H. L. Brown
Treasurer	Sol Karet

1917 - 1922
President	Benjamin Drage
Vice President	H. M. Lush
Treasurer	Sol Karet
Hon. secretary	Joseph Hyams
Board of Management	Benjamin Drage, Mr H. M Lush, Sol Karet, Joseph Hyams, L. Bernstein, Montague Jacobs, A. Bloch, R. Katz, G. Cohen, H. Kerman, J. Davies, L. Lubin, S. Drage, J. M. Maurice, Paul Goodman, J. Samuel, M. Greidinger, Jimmy Seaford, F. Hieger and A. L. Victor

Jacob Greenbaum

1922 (May to November)
Wardens	Benjamin Drage, Mr H. M Lush
Financial Representative	Sol Karet

1922 – 1924
Wardens	Benjamin Drage and Joseph Hymans
Financial Representative	Sol Karet

1924 – 1925
Wardens	Joseph Hymans and Jimmy Seaford
Financial Representative	Sol Karet

1925 – 1926
Wardens	Joseph Hymans and Jimmy Seaford
Financial Representative	Councillor J. W. Rosenthal
Board of Management	L. Bernstein, Jacob Greenbaum, M. Greidinger, L. Hyams, A. Jacobs, Sol Karet, Mr M.P. Kempner, Jimmy Seaford and A. W. Woolf

Morris Laufer

1926 – 1928
Wardens	Joseph Hymans and Councillor J. D. Somper, JP
Financial Representative	Councillor J. W. Rosenthal

1928 – 1929

Wardens	Councillor J. D. Somper, JP and L. Hyams
Financial representative	Jacob Greenbaum
Board of Management	Messrs S. Bolsom, E. Goldston, A. Jacobs, Sol Karet, O. Philipp, J. Samuel, Jimmy Seaford, L. Silverblatt and M. Wix

1929 – 1931

Wardens	Jacob Greenbaum and Philip Jacobs
Financial representative	Alderman S. Bolsom, JP

1932 – 1933

Wardens	Philip Jacobs and S. London
Financial representative	Alderman S. Bolsom, JP

1933 – 1934

Wardens	Alderman Bolsom, JP and Mr S. London
Financial representative	S. Josephs
Board of Management	Messrs L. Bernstein, Sidney Ellis, E. Goldston, Jacob Greenbaum, H. Hyman, A. Jacobs, P. Jacobs, Sol Karet, J. Samuel and S. Werner

1935

Wardens	Alderman Bolsom, JP and Mr S. London
Financial representative	S. Josephs
Board of Management	Messrs J. Bloch, Sidney Ellis, L. Elton, E. Goldston, Jacob Greenbaum, H. Hyman, P. Jacobs, Sol Karet, I. Kestenbaum, Morris Laufer, J. Nadler, B. Rappaport and S. Werner

1936 – 1937

Wardens	Alderman Bolsom, JP and Mr M. Freedman
Financial representative	Sol Karet

1937 – 1938

Wardens	Myer Freedman, H. Hyman
Financial representative	Sol Karet
Board of Management	Messrs J. Bloch, Councillor S. Bolsom, S. Goldstein, E. Goldston, Jacob Greenbaum, S. Josephs, Morris Laufer, D. Levene, S. London and Arthur Taylor

1938 – 1939

Wardens	Myer Freedman, H. Hyman
Financial representative	Sol Karet

1939 – 1940

Wardens	H. Hyman and Sol Karet
Financial representative	Arthur Taylor
Board of Management:	Councillor S. Bolsom, Messrs. L. Elton, M. Freedman, S. Goldstein, E. Goldston, Jacob Greenbaum, H. Jacobs, S. Josephs, John Landau, Morris Laufer and S. London

1940 – 1941

Wardens	H. Hyman and Mr S. Josephs
Financial representative	Arthur Taylor

1941 – 1943

Wardens	Mr S. Josephs and Mr H. Jacobs
Financial representative	Arthur Taylor

1943 – 1945
Wardens   Mr H. Jacobs and Arthur Taylor
Financial representative   Alfred Woolf

1945 – 1947
Wardens   Arthur Taylor and Alfred Woolf
Financial representative   Councillor Charles Barclay

1947 – 1949
Wardens   Alfred Woolf and Charles Barclay, JP
Financial representative   Michael Horne

1949 – 1951
Wardens   Alfred Woolf and Charles Barclay, JP
Financial representative   Michael Horne

Bruno Marmorstein

1951 – 1953
Wardens   Charles Barclay, JP and Barnet Beckman
Financial representative   Myer Harris

1953 – 1954
Wardens: Barnet Beckman and Myer Harris
Financial representative   Bruno Marmorstein

1954 – 1955
Secretary   Harry Ward
Wardens   Barnet Beckman and Myer Harris Harris
Financial representative   Morris Laufer
Board of Management   Norman Bloom, Sidney Boder, Jack Bogush, Seymour Craig, Jacob Greenbaum, Rev Joseph Halpern, Philip Haltrecht, Harry Levine, Jimmy Seaford, Arthur Taylor, Dr Sidney Torrance, Hyman Verbov, Alfred Woolf

1955 – 1957
Wardens   Myer Harris and Morris Laufer
Financial representative   Robert Epstein

1957 – 1958
Wardens   Morris Laufer and Robert Epstein
Financial representative   Seymour Craig

1958 – 1959
Wardens   Mr M. Laufer and Seymour Craig
Financial representative   Michael Balin

1959 – 1960
Wardens   Seymour Craig and Michael Balin
Financial representative   Ian Hershman

Joseph Hyams

1961 – 1963
Secretary   Harry S. Ward
Wardens   Seymour Craig and Michael Balin
Financial representative   Ian Hershman
Board of Management   Judah Blackman, Philip Cohen, B. A. Cowan, Jacques Daniels, Jacob Greenbaum, David Levene, Samuel Miller, Samuel Mitzman, Jacob E. Perlow, S. Rosen, Harry A. Samuels and Dr Sidney Torrance

1963 – 1965
Wardens | Michael Balin and Ian Hershman
Financial representative | Philip Cohen
Board of Management | Mr. B. A. Cowan, Mr. S. Craig, Mr. J. Greenbaum, Mr F. Ellis Lincoln, Samuel Miller, Mr. S. Mitzman, Mr. S. Rosen, Mr. H. A. Samuels, Dr. L. J. Samuels MC, Sidney Schreiber, Mr. H. Wasser, Dr Ernest Woolf

1965 – 1967
Wardens | Ian Hershman and Philip Cohen
Financial representative | Benjamin Rose

1967 – 1968
Wardens | Philip Cohen and Benjamin Rose
Financial representative | Sidney Torrance

1968 – 1970
Wardens | Benjamin Rose and Sidney Torrance
Financial representative | Simon Rurka

1970 – 1971
Wardens | Benjamin Rose and Sidney Torrance
Financial representative | Simon Rurka

1971 – 1973
Wardens | Sidney Torrance and Simon Rurka
Financial representative | Judah Blackman
Board of Management | Sidney Boder, Dr Arnold Cohen, Philip Cohen, Ralph Cohen, David Gedalla, M. Jacobs, I. Lerner, Sidney Palace, E. Palmer, M. Rose, David Shapiro, Montague Teff

1973 – 1975
Secretary | Harry S. Ward
Wardens | Judah Blackman and David Gedalla
Financial representative | J. Asher Blau

1975 – 1976
Secretary | Harry Ward
Wardens | David Gedalla and Cecil Oberman
Financial representative | Leslie M. Green

1976 – 1977
Secretary | Harry Ward
Wardens | Leslie M. Green and Prof. Albert Neuberger, CBE
Financial representative | David Gedalla

1977 – 1978
Secretary | Harry Ward
Wardens: | Leslie M. Green and David Gedalla
Financial representative | Edward Conway
Board of Management: | Messrs Sidney Boder, Philip Cohen, Ralph Cohen, David Crossley, M. Jacobs, Michael Martin, Alan Mays, Samuel Mitzman, Sidney Palace, M. Rose, David Shapiro and Benjamin Taite

1978 – 1979
Secretary | Harry Ward
Wardens | Leslie M. Green and David Gedalla
Financial representative | Edward Conway

1979 – 1980
Secretary   Harry Ward
Wardens   Leslie M. Green and Edward Conway
Financial representative   David Gedalla

1980 – 1981
Warden   Leslie M. Green
Financial representative   Gabriel White

1981 – 1983
Warden   Leslie M. Green and Gabriel White
Financial representative   David Crossley

1983 – 1984
Warden   Gabriel White and David Shapiro
Financial representative   Morris Woolf

1984 – 1985
Warden   Leslie Green and David Crossley
Financial representative   Morris Woolf

1985 – November 1988
Warden   Leslie Green and David Shapiro
Financial representative   Morris Woolf

November 1988 – May 1989
Warden   Leslie Green and Abraham Bernstein
Financial representative   Morris Woolf

1989 – 1990
Warden   Leslie Green and Abraham Bernstein

1990 – 1991
Warden   Leslie Green and Mr I. Freiberger (acting warden)

1991 – 1993
Warden   Leslie Green and Mr I. Freiberger
Financial representative   David Tarlow (from December 1922)

1993 – 1995
Warden   Philip Solomons and Saul Morris
Financial representative   David Tarlow

1995 – 1996
Chairman   Robin Summers
Vice chairman   Paul Shaerf
Warden   Philip Solomons and Stephen Shaw
Financial representative   David Tarlow

1996 – 1997
Chairman   Robin Summers
Vice chairman   Paul Shaerf
Warden   Philip Solomons and Stephen Shaw
Financial representative   David Tarlow

1997 – 1998

Chairman   Robin Summers
Warden   Philip Solomons
Financial representative   David Tarlow

1998 – 1999

Chairman   Robin Summers
Wardens   Philip Solomons and Terence Sopel
Financial representative   David Tarlow

1999 – 2000

Chairman   Peter Zinkin
Wardens   Joe Friedman and Terence Sopel
Financial representative   Dr Simon Cohen

2000 – 2001

Chairman   Peter Zinkin
Warden   Joe Friedman
Financial representative   Dr Simon Cohen

2001 – 2005

Chairman   Peter Zinkin
Vice Chairman   Jackie Crossley
Wardens   Joe Friedman and Benny Chain
Financial representative   Philip Goodman

2005 – 2006

Vice Chairman   Jackie Crossley
Warden   Benny Chain
Financial representative   Philip Goodman

2006 – 2007

Vice Chairman   Jacqui Zinkin
Financial representative   Philip Goodman

2007 – 2008

Vice Chairman   Jacqui Zinkin
Wardens   Dr Rob Ginsburg, Julian Goodkin
Financial Representative   Alberto Ottolenghi
Honorary Officer   Jeremy Manuel, OBE

2008 – 2010

Vice Chairman   Jacqui Zinkin
Wardens   Dr Rob Ginsburg, Julian Goodkin
Financial Representative   Adrian Jacobs
Honorary Officer   Paul Morland

2010 – 2011

Chairman   Benny Chain
Vice Chairman   Jacqui Zinkin
Wardens: Dr Rob Ginsburg, Julian Goodkin
Financial Representative   Adrian Jacobs
Honorary Officer   Paul Morland

APPENDIX 1 - OFFICERS OF THE CONGREGATION

2011 – 2012

Chairman	Benny Chain
Vice Chairman	Jacqui Zinkin
Wardens	Julian Goodkin
Financial Representative	Jonathan Davies
Honorary Officer	Paul Morland

2012 – 2013

Chairman	Benny Chain
Vice Chairman	Peter Zinkin
Wardens	Julian Goodkin
Financial Representative	Jonathan Davies
Honorary Officer	Paul Morland

2013 – 2014

Chairman	Benny Chain
Vice Chairman	Peter Zinkin
Wardens	Dr Rob Ginsburg, Terry Sopel
Financial Representative	Jonathan Davies

2014 – 2015

Vice Chairman	Peter Zinkin
Wardens	Dr Rob Ginsburg, Terry Sopel
Financial Representative	Jonathan Davies

2015 – 2016

Chairman	Peter Zinkin
Vice Chairman	Jackie Crossley
Warden	Terry Sopel
Financial Representative	Jonathan Davies

Marriage Registers: 1919-1929

26 October 1919 – Solomon Lewis, civil servant (admiralty), son of Samuel Myer Lewis to Nathalie Neudorf, daughter of Adolf Neudorf (diamond merchant). Married in Golders Green Synagogue.

9 June 1920 – Maurice Katzner, manager (Wholesale Clothiers), son of Samuel Katzner, to Catherine Rosalie Fuld, daughter of Julians Fuld (merchant), married Frascati Restaurant, 32 Oxford Street.

7 June 1921 – Solomon Matthew Robinson, Skin dresser, son of Myer Robinson (teacher), to Evelyn Burnford, daughter of Moses Samuel Bernstein (deceased) married at Devonshire Hall, Hackney

17 December 1922 – Sydney Cohen, Commercial traveller, son of Ted Cohen (government contractor), to Celia Mindel, daughter of Cecil Mindel (tailor) marred at Golders Green Synagogue

4 February 1923 – Max Klein, farrier, son of Harris Klein (deceased), to Leiba (Lily) Brilliant, milliner, daughter of Joseph Brilliant, tailor, married at Golders Green Synagogue.

16 April 1923 – Oscar Felix Rilter, widower, ironmonger, Son of Moses Ritter (deceased) to Rebecca Esenberg, daughter of Woolf Esenberg (tailor), married in The Empress Hall, East End

17 June 1923 – Jack Lipman, Shoe manufacturer, son of Isaac Lipman (Shoe manufacturer) to Amelia Swyers, daughter of David Swyers (mortgage broker), married at Golders Green Synagogue

Marriage of Queenie Finegold to Harvey Cyzer.

25 July 1923 – Lionel Charles Goldsmith, manager (house furnishings), son of Jacob Goldsmith (deceased) to Muriel Alge, daughter of Jacob Alge (deceased), married at Holborn Restaurant, High Holborn

21 August 1923 – Hyman Fox, dental surgeon, son of Mark Fax (deceased), to Lydia Rose Abravanel, daughter of Salvador Abravanel (company manager), married Golders Green Synagogue

4 November 1923 – Victor Alexander, master tailor, son of Alexander Wergrovsky (master tailor) to Esther Myers, daughter of Simon Myers (tobacconist), married in Golders Green Synagogue.

9 December 1923 – Samuel Lesopky, manufacturer, son of Nathan Lesopky (gentleman) to Leah Fish, daughter of Israel Fish (gentleman), married in Golders Green Synagogue.

5 February 1924 – Joseph Lewin (commercial agent, hatters), son of Herman Lewin (merchant), to Yvonne Block, daughter of Ormand Block (merchant), married Golders Green Synagogue, witnessed by Asher Littenberg and Mendel Susser

10 February 1924 – Isaac Bertram Miller, Commercial traveller, son of Mark Miller (tailor), to Pear Taflowitch Walker, daughter of Isaac Taflowitch Walker (tailor), married in Golders Green Synagogue.

23 March 1924 – Jacob Kravetsky, tailor, son of Chargin Kravetsky (deceased), to Janie Landsberg, Secretary, daughter of Louise Landsberg (deceased), married at Golders Green Synagogue

5 June 1924 – Joseph Cohen, wine and spirit merchant, son of Alexander Cohen (merchant), to Clara Toledano, (otherwise Daniels), daughter of Joshua Daniels, musician.

10 June 1924 – Newman Morris, clothier, son of Walter Morris (clothier), to Reka Grant, daughter of Hyman Grant (manufacturer)

25 June 1924 – Albert Hart, manufacturer ladies apparel, son of Bernard Hart (deceased) to Esther Gordon, daughter of Maurice Gordon (merchant)

16 July 1924 – Harry Curtis, (mantle manufacturer), to Hilda Goldstein, daughter of Lewis Goldstein (mantle manufacturer)

12 August 1924 – Marks Plotkin, widower, jeweller, son of Uri Plotkin (deceased) to Doris Esther Kremer (formerly Kamm), formerly the wife of Norman Kremer from whom she obtained a divorce, daughter of Marcus Kamm (dentist)

Wedding of Lionel and Helen Manuel, 12 June 1949.

12 August 1924 – Jack Harris (representative of a company) son of Jacob Harris (deceased) to Babs Leah Glassman, daughter of Maurice Glassman (picture frame maker)

25 September 1924 – Louis Hirsch Penn, assistant to the trades commissioner for South Africa in London, so of Solomon Penn (merchant) to Dora Jacobson, daughter of Solomon Jacobson (merchant)

20 January 1925 – Harold Benjamin Cannon, Ladies tailor, son of Jacob Cannon, Ladies tailor, son of Jacob Cannon (master tailor), to Betty Bernstein, daughter of Lazarus Bernstein (furrier)

17 February 1925 – Solomon Lefkowitz, produce merchant, son of Lewis Lefkowitz (produce merchant), to Eva Gordon, daughter of Neilon Gordon (deceased)

17 March 1925 – Harry Randall, furniture manufacturer, son of Isaac Randall (cabinet manufacturer) to Rose Muriel Freedman, daughter of Joseph Freedman (furniture dealer)

26 May 1925 – Eugen Mayer, merchant, son f Heinrich Mayer (deceased), to Beatrice Amalie Haliener (widow), daughter of Adolph Simon (merchant)

8 July 1925 – Samuel Bril, painter, son of Hartog Bril (deceased) to *Hannah* Julie Ramus, daughter of Aubrey Ramus (art dealer)

21 July 1925 – Samuel Henry Baron, cloth manufacturer, son of Joachim Hyan Baron (woollen merchant) to Alice Foulds, daughter of Robert Foulds (deceased)

27 December 1925 – Abraham Liebling, draper, son of Lewis Liebling (draper) to Annie Brazil, daughter of Alec Brazil (cabinet maker)

19 January 1926 – Leizer Preger, mantle manufacturers agent, son of Alexander Leizer (contractor) to Doris Lushinski, daughter of Henry Lushinski (manufacturer)

24 May 1926 – Felix Jacobs, Ladies Clothing, son of Arthur Jacobs (merchant) to Rita Rebecca Lubin, Secretary to ladies clothing company, daughter of Louis Lubin (leather merchant)

4 October 1926 – George Schildkraut, engraver, son of Lazarus Schildkraut (deceased) to Bella Miriam Karet, daughter of Jacob Karet (merchant ironmonger)

7 December 1926 – Jacob Wolf Rosenthal, widower, theatre proprietor, son of Isaac Rosenthal (gentleman) to Ethen Friend, accountant, daughter of Henry Friend (sponge merchant)

19 December 1926 – Jack Schwartz, suitcase manufacturer, son of David Schwatz (deceased) to Lillie Jacobs, daughter of Abraham Jacobs (cloth merchant)

26 June 1927 – Albert Malin, cabinet maker, son of Benjamin Malin (furniture manufacturer) to Irene Littenberg, daughter of Asher Littenberg (minister of religion)

Marriage of Monroe Palmer and Susette Hall.

19 September 1927 – Harold Meek, accountant, son of Julius Meek (caterer of confectioner) to Helena Lushinski, daughter of Henry Lushinski (manufacturer)

25 October 1927 – Myer Weisblatt, master hosier, son of Abraham Weisblatt (boot and shoe manufacturer) to Lily Black, daughter of Joseph Black (caterer)

27 December 1927 – Geoffrey Kalis, dealer in wireless accessories, son of Isaac Kalisky (General Merchant) to Phyllis Pearl, daughter of Morris Pearl (wireless dealer)

1 February 1928 – Harold Samuels, wholesale jeweller, son of Barnet Samuels (manufacturer) to Ethel Elizabeth Popper, daughter of William Popper (printer)

25 March 1928 – Ernest Harris Silverstone, Solicitor, son of Robert Silverstone (manufacturers agent) to Hetty Fishstein (otherwise fisher), daughter of Judah Fishstein (deceased)

25 March 1928 – Largan Bravo, general merchant, son of Jacob Bravo (deceased) to the Ita Szac, dental surgeon daughter of Nahum Szac (deceased)

19 June 1928 – Lewis Woolf, garage proprietor, son of John Woolf (wholesale fruitier) to Katherine Leah Isaacs, daughter of Albert Isaacs (antique dealer)

21 June 1928 – Alfred Martyn, director of clothing company, son of Herman Marchinski (deceased) to Millie Ophelia Jackson, daughter of Charles William Jackson (deceased)

1 July 1928 – John Saphra, leather goods merchant, son of Julius Saphra (gentleman) to Kathleen Mary Goldschmidt, daughter of Hermann Goldschmidt (stockbroker)

Paul Lang's marriage to Verna Shisler, 7 March 1989.
COURTESY DAVID LANG

29 July 1928 – Henry Solomon Libstein, commercial traveller, son of Abraham Libstein (deceased) to Eileen Marjorie Davis, daughter of Ralph Davis (gentleman)

12 August 1928 – Emile Schnabel, merchant, son of Charles Schnabeet (gentleman), to Figa Bertha Feld, daughter of Louis Feld (merchant)

29 August 1928 – Wolfe Maximilian Snapper, lace manufacturer, son of David Snapper (deceased) to Mabel (Molly) Cohen, daughter of Lewis Cohen (general warehouseman)

4 September 1928 – Reginald George Napier, Steel merchant, son of Moses Myer Napier (general dealer) to Vera Constance Erman, daughter of David Erdman (general warehouseman)

Wedding of Monroe Palmer.

9 September 1928 – Marks Peretz, upholster, son of Marcus Peretz (deceased) to Rebecca Glassman, insurance agent, daughter of Abraham Moses Glassman (deceased)

14 October 1928 – Charles Lewis, commercial traveller, son of Abraham Lewis (merchant tailor) to Lily Zelin (widow), salesman, daughter of Harris Karet

12 December 1928 – Bernard (Harry) Simmonds, toy manufacturer, son of Abraham Simmonder (toy manufacturer) to Rose Yager, daughter of Harry Yager (cabinet manufacturer)

3 January 1929 – Samuel Isaacs Phillips, gentleman's out fitters, son of Hyman Isaacs (outfitter) to Ena Berg, daughter of Herman Berg (furnisher)

13 January 1929 – Hyman Pearl, wireless dealer, son of Morris Pearl (deceased) to Eva Evelyn Brook, daughter of Abraham Brook (deceased)

15 January 1929 – Joseph Maurice Slot, of Independent Means, son of Solomon Slot (gentleman) of 8 Carlton Mansions, West Kensington to Marie Hyams, daughter of Lewis Hymans (manufacturer)

27 January 1929 – Harry Settloff, ladies outfitter, son of Jacob Settloff (ladies outfitter) to Gladys Muriel Jacobs, daughter of Joseph David Jacobs (Solicitor)

17 February 1929 – Jack Markus, commercial traveller, son of Max Marks (Robe Manufacturer), to Ada Bella Apple, daughter of Lazarus Apple (wireless wholesaler)

17 February 1929 – Montague Woolf, tailor, son of Joseph Woolf (clothier) to Elizabeth Bloomfield, daughter of Elias Bloomfield (clothing contractor)

31 March 1929 – Maurice Wyndham Weinrabe, bankrupt stock buyer, son of Jacob Weinrabe (stock buyer) to June Violet Emanuel, daughter of Edward Emanuel (printer)

7 April 1929 – Scholam Nelson, company director, son of Harry Nelson (caterer) to Winifred Leah Phillips, daughter of Charles Phillips (merchant grocer)

10 April 1929 – Solomon Yager, timber salesman, son of Harry Yager (company director) to Ettie Tobias, daughter of Soloman Tobias (fur skin dresser)

17 April 1929 – Harold Joseph Fraser, hotel inspector, son of Loouis Fraser (clerk) to Winifred Alice Levy, daughter of Thomas Levy (company director)

17 June 1929 – Sydney Rose, outfitter, son of Lewis Rose (clothier) to Theresa Roth, private secretary, daughter of Alexander Roth (deceased)

23 June 1929 – Hyman Harold Grant, Chartered Accountant, son of Philip Grant (hat manufacturer) to Isabel Ornstien, bank clerk, daughter of Phineas Orstein (deceased)

10 July 1929 – Gersham Asbrahamson, Insurance Clerk, son of Joseph Abrahamson (tailor) to Rachel Levy, bank clerk, daughter of Morris Levy (deceased)

25 August 1929 – Maurice Raphael White, wholesale clothing manufacturer, son of Samuel White (gentleman) to Anne Wienstein, private secretary, daughter of Harris Wienstein (tobacconist)

1 October 1929 – John Isaacs Phillips, gentleman outfitters, son of Hyman Isaacs Phillips (outfitters) to Leah Berg, daughter of Herman Berg (furnisher)

A page from the marriage register during World War Two.

Index